W9-CBI-773

Week-by-Week Homework for Building
Reading Comprehension and Fluency

30 Reproducible High-Interest Passages for Kids to Read Aloud at Home—With Companion Activities

GRADES 2–3

BY MARY ROSE

New York • Toronto • London • Auckland • Sydney
Mexico City • New Delhi • Hong Kong • Buenos Aires

Teaching *Resources*

DEDICATION

To Marietta Huckeba, the best friend Lake Sybelia ever had

ACKNOWLEDGMENTS

Special thanks to Tom Rose, my ever patient husband

And further special thanks to Maxine Efstathion, Kate Raleigh, and John Rowland of Lake Sybelia Elementary School and to story contributors Susan Seay and Shannon Crawford

Thanks also to Terry Cooper, Joanna Davis-Swing, and Merryl Maleska Wilbur of Scholastic Inc.

CREDITS

"The Fire on the Mountain," rewritten by Mary Rose. Originally from *The Fire on the Mountain* by Harold Courlander and Wolf Leslau. © 1950 by Holt, Rinehart and Winston.

"The History of Gum" is reprinted from the April/May 2002 issue of STORYWORKS magazine. Copyright © 2002 by Scholastic Inc. Reprinted by permission of Scholastic Inc.

"Let's Marry! said the Cherry" by N.M. Bodecker is reprinted from *Let's Marry! said the Cherry and Other Nonsense Poems* by N.M. Bodecker. Copyright © 1974 by N.M. Bodecker.

"Rain Sizes" by John Ciardi from THE REASON FOR THE PELICAN by John Ciardi. Copyright © 1955 by Curtis Publishing Co.

"The Spaghetti Challenge" by Leslie D. Perkins from A BAD CASE OF THE GIGGLES by Bruce Lansky. Published by Meadowbrook Press, 1994.

"Spaghetti! Spaghetti!" by Jack Prelutsky is reprinted from RAINY, RAINY SATURDAY by Jack Prelutsky. Copyright © 1980 by Jack Prelutsky. Used by permission of HarperCollins Publishers.

"December Leaves" by Kaye Starbird from DON'T EVER CROSS A CROCODILE by Kaye Starbird. Copyright © 1963 by Kaye Starbird and renewed 1991. Reprinted by permission of Marian Reiner.

Every effort has been made to acquire permission to use the materials in this book.

Research cited is based on information in:

Allington, Richard L. *What Really Matters for Struggling Reader.* New York: Addison Wesley Longman, 2001.

Allington, Richard L. and Patricia M. Cunningham. *Schools That Work: Where All Children Read and Write.* New York: HarperCollins, 1996.

Cover design by Jason Robinson
Interior design by Solutions by Design, Inc.
Interior illustrations (fiction and poetry) by Maxie Chambliss
Interior illustrations (nonfiction) by Teresa Southwell

ISBN: 0-439-51779-6

Copyright © 2004 by Mary Rose
Published by Scholastic Inc.
All rights reserved.
Printed in the U.S.A.

22 23 24   40   24 23 22 21 20 19 18 17

Contents

Introduction

In 1999, facing a fourth-grade classroom of struggling readers, I came up with a homework project aimed at increasing the amount of time my students spent reading aloud. A great deal of research (Allington and Cunningham) has shown that students need far more "read out loud" experiences than the typical classroom can give them. Each week, I assigned my students at the Lake Sybelia Elementary School in Maitland, Florida, a passage to read out loud at home to an adult, along with a set of questions to answer. Each of the questions was directly tied to a state standard or benchmark for language arts. To make it easier for parents to be part of the teaching process, I addressed a letter to them each week explaining the assignment so they could better assist their child.

This concept proved to be so successful that I shared it in workshops with other teachers across the country. Eventually, the book *Week-by-Week Homework for Building Reading Comprehension and Fluency, Grades 3–6* (Scholastic, 2002) evolved. Classroom teachers in those grades found it so helpful that a miniseries has now come about—a similar book aimed at Grade 1, along with *this* book, which is specifically targeted to readers in second and third grades.

This book, like the others, is set up as a series of discrete assignments, each consisting of a short reading passage, a letter to the parents, and questions to be answered. There are thirty lessons, intended to offer teachers homework options for every week of the heart of the academic year. In the broadest sense, my hope is that these homework assignments can meet a variety of needs—from those of any beginning reader to those of older, struggling readers, as well as adults who may be learning English as a second language.

Why Silent Reading Isn't Enough

As young readers build their skills, their teachers are tempted to allow them to complete more and more reading assignments with silent reading. Yes, sustained silent reading is highly effective in developing students' reading ability and increasing their motivation, and yes, children learn to read by reading—but beware! Often, though young students *appear* quite fluent as they're reading silently, they are not reading effectively, and their comprehension is poor. In fact, they often fail to use many of the word attack and comprehension skills we have tried to teach them.

Following is a list of the major pitfalls and shortcomings of silent reading:

- Silent reading allows students to read quickly, often causing them to miss the main idea of the passage.

- Silent reading allows students to skip words they do not know. Skipping unfamiliar words is often taught as a good reading strategy, and indeed it is. But it is only a good strategy if the student rereads the sentence and tries to figure out the unknown word through context or syntactic clues. We cannot tell if children reread for meaning when they are reading silently. We suspect that good readers do reread, but poorer readers, who need it the most, often do not.

○ Silent reading allows children to mispronounce words, which hampers their comprehension. Students wind up maintaining misconceptions about text, and teachers have no way of knowing that these misconceptions even exist. A student who routinely goes fishing and has seen her father filet a fish many times is still likely to read *filet* incorrectly. This is a familiar word in her oral vocabulary, but not in her reading vocabulary. When a teacher hears a child mispronounce a word, it is an opportunity to help the student connect written and oral words.

○ Silent reading does not teach children to read with expression, to use voice inflections, or to adjust the rate of reading to reflect the content. Thus, they miss out on a great deal, such as the excitement of a story as it builds to a climax.

○ Silent reading offers teachers no information about the child's awareness of punctuation. On their own, many young readers just go along calling out words without pauses for periods or attention to quotation marks.

○ Silent reading does not encourage children to listen to themselves as they read, a habit which helps them to correct their errors and to insure that what they read makes sense.

Classroom Strategies for Maximizing Read-Aloud Experiences

While the subject of this book is increasing your students' oral reading skills through at-home work, let's first take a quick look at a few effective classroom strategies also aimed at augmenting read-aloud time. The two approaches— in-class reading and out-of-class reading—are merely different arenas for meeting the same instructional goals. The seven classroom reading strategies described below avoid "round-robin" reading and are nonthreatening to poor readers.

1. **Reread familiar passages.** Read a passage one day and have students read the same passage the following day.

2. **Read old favorites.** Remember when you were young (and perhaps when your own children were young) and the best thing about reading was hearing the same stories over and over and over again? Why is it that, as teachers, we say, "You read that last year, we can't use it again in the third grade"? Students often get more out of the story a second or third time through, and once familiar with a text, even struggling readers are less embarrassed to read out loud. When students are reading an old favorite, they tend to be smoother and use great voice inflections. Keep this in mind as the year progresses; go

back and reread stories that have become familiar to students and thus much easier for them to handle.

3. **Choral reading.** This is a particularly effective strategy for reading poetry. Try a variety of poems—poems that are funny, that tell a story, that have a delightful rhythm or are read in two parts or have deep meaning. Read the poems several times over to help students feel the rhyme or clarify meaning.

4. **Paired reading.** In this technique, students in pairs or groups of three are scattered around the classroom. There are a number of effective and fun variations possible. One child can read the narration while the other reads the dialogue; they can take turns reading the parts of the characters; they can switch off so they alternate reading a whole page or a whole paragraph; or one child can read a whole chapter or short story one day and switch roles the next day. We tend to do this kind of activity with fiction, but it is great with nonfiction, too

5. **Reading buddies.** Pair students with younger-grade children and have them read picture books to their little buddies. Most popular picture books are written for young children, but actually contain sophisticated literary devices and require a high level of reading skill.

6. **Read plays.** This technique is particularly effective when you discuss the play and assign parts ahead of time. In this way, a child can practice his or her part until it flows fluently and he or she feels comfortable with voice inflections and word meanings. Students also tend to pay extra attention when reading plays because they want to be ready when their turn to read comes.

7. **Have students read their own writing out loud to the class.** Many state standards for language arts include listening and speaking. You can build your students' confidence in their reading and writing abilities by giving them time to read their own essays, reports, or stories out loud to the rest of the class.

Easy-to-Use Homework Routine

As described earlier, the series of homework assignments in this book addresses the need for more oral reading practice and capitalizes on the enthusiasm of parents. Each week students receive a short passage to read aloud to their parents or caregivers. Then they answer a few related questions. A letter to parents, which includes instructional tips and guidelines for the reading and the questions, is part of each take-home lesson. Finally, both parent and child sign the homework page, indicating that they worked together on the assignment. The relevant skill for the lesson is highlighted at the top of the right-hand page of each lesson. Introduce the homework routine to parents with a letter like the one on page 11.

There is no order in which you should use these lessons. You might decide to use them chronologically, but more likely, you will pick and choose selections and their accompanying skill reinforcement activities to complement the teaching you are doing in a particular week. You might also select lessons that reflect themes or holidays (see, for example, comments at the beginning of Chapter 4).

Here are some advantages to this easy-to-use homework routine:

○ **Children have ample time to complete the assignment.** Giving students an entire school week to turn in the homework removes a great deal of pressure from busy families. Many parents find that they are more likely to help with the work if it can be done at their own convenience.

○ **There is no expense involved.** Unlike many other parent projects that require expensive purchases, training nights, make-and-take games, and follow-up charts, this project gets all the parents involved at virtually no cost.

○ **Parents become aware of their child's reading ability.** Many parents do not have a real sense of the nature of the reading materials their child can handle nor of their child's reading level.

○ **Students get credit, but not a grade, for returning the signed homework page.** This low-pressure evaluation means that you can quickly scan the returned pages and give "credit" or "no credit" marks, enabling you to focus on the far more important job of giving positive feedback to both parents and students. Mark the papers with comments, smiles, stars, or stickers to encourage both parents and children to continue with the work. Do not display a chart in the classroom indicating which students have returned their homework. This is very discouraging for those whose families will not or cannot help them. Evaluations should be private information in your grade book.

○ **Students see the assignments as a continuation of the work they do in school, not simply as "busy work" or homework for homework's sake.** The practice reinforces the teaching you're doing and the content is relevant to your classroom lessons. Incidentally, many of the articles in this book can be used to support science and social studies curriculums.

Benefits of This Routine for Teachers, Parents, and Beginning Readers

Teachers everywhere are looking for simple ways to make their teaching lives easier while maintaining high-quality instruction. They want homework that is easily graded, yet meaningful to the child and relevant to the curriculum. Teachers need to find homework assignments that will help them reinforce mandated state assessment benchmarks, but they often must scramble to do so.

Parents everywhere appreciate homework that they understand, that reinforces concepts being taught in school, that is easy to complete, and that is sensitive to their busy schedules. They want to be reassured that the work their child is doing is meaningful to the child and relevant to the local curriculum and state assessment standards.

Students everywhere are tired of repetitious, uninteresting skill-and-drill practice sheets. They are very willing to complete assignments that are easy to understand and that deal with subjects of interest to them. And many young readers are delighted by assignments that require interaction with busy parents, providing them a moment in the spotlight to show off their new skills.

- **The skills practiced are correlated to national reading standards.** Parents become aware of the skills that will eventually be tested on state and national exams in the higher grades. Teachers can look at these standards to make sure they are covering everything that is expected of them.

- **The assignments are instant homework.** Instead of having to hunt for or create meaningful assignments correlated to your curriculum, you can simply reproduce these standards-based activities.

- **The homework encourages communication between parents and teacher.** Parents receive a letter from you every week, helping them feel connected to what's going on in their child's classroom.

- **The thirty homework lessons provided in this book help parents support your teaching throughout the year.** Each passage is accompanied by an explanatory Parent Letter, thus helping parents to be aware of and reinforce your work in the classroom.

> ### Reading Standards addressed in this book
>
> **The student . . .**
>
> determines the main idea of the text.
>
> identifies relevant supporting details.
>
> arranges events in chronological order.
>
> recognizes cause-and-effect relationships.
>
> recognizes the use of compare and contrast.
>
> recognizes similarities and differences in characters, settings and events in a story.
>
> recognizes differences in fact and opinion.
>
> identifies author's purpose.
>
> compares works of literature to each other.
>
> makes connections between text and graphic illustrations.
>
> constructs meaning from complex reading selections.
>
> uses context clues.
>
> makes predictions before and during reading.
>
> makes inferences and draws conclusions from story elements.
>
> recognizes parts of speech.
>
> understands and interprets figurative language.
>
> clarifies understanding by reading and self-correction.
>
> recognizes the effects of language such as sensory words, rhymes and word patterns.
>
> recognizes root words, prefixes, and suffixes and knows how they change the meaning of a word.
>
> uses literary terminology such as *theme* and *simile*.
>
> identifies synonyms in context.

Hints for Success

Following is a list of guidelines to help you implement the homework routine in this book:

- Pass out these homework assignments on the same day each week. (Mine go home on Mondays.)

- Allow until the end of the week to complete the work. (My students are allowed to turn in work any day up to and including Friday.)

- Insist that both the parent and the child sign at the top of the page. Return unsigned papers to the parent for a signature before you will accept them.

- Give credit (or partial credit), but not a grade, for completing homework. (I give full credit, half credit, or no credit checkmarks in my grade book.)

- Make exceptions when needed. (I had one parent who worked nights through the week. I chose to accept her child's homework on Mondays so that she could help him complete it over the weekend.) The key points are that the assignment is considered important and that it is done correctly.

- Assign homework "behind your teaching." This means that when you pass out a homework assignment, it should cover a skill that you have already taught. If you assign homework on a skill that you only introduced earlier that day, students may feel frustrated at home because neither they nor their parents quite know how to do the work. If you assign something that the child already understands, the homework will go much more smoothly for the child and the parent. Generally speaking, homework should be a review or practice of skills already learned. Parents should not be expected to do the teaching at home.

- Introduce the homework routine to parents with a letter like the one on page 11.

Assessment Made Easy

Most teachers are busy with an overwhelming load of papers to grade and plans to write. Save yourself time and effort by using this simple method of assessing homework. The method works especially well when you are unsure of the amount of help the child received from an adult. Consider giving credit, partial credit, or no credit for these assignments. Skimming the answers will tell you if the child has actually read the story and understood the questions. Indicate this in your grade book with a check, a horizontal line, or a zero. When the grading period ends, use a homework grade to help you decide the child's letter grade for the period. If you gave eight assignments during the term, students who successfully completed and returned at least seven get an A for homework; students that did at least six get a B; five a C; four a D; and three or fewer, an F.

Offer a second chance. Occasionally you will have a parent who did not understand the passage or was unable to assist the child. Consider a phone call or a note to the parent to clarify things, and give the child a second chance to get the assignment right. The parents will love you for this—and remember, the goal of this project is to help children become better readers. If they totally missed the main message or skills presented in the passage, this means they did not understand it. Give them a second chance to get it right.

Dear Parents,

Reading well is a key to success in school, on state and national tests, and in life in general. Students need to be able to read fluently and with expression. They must be able to get information from what they have read, and they must be able to respond to literature. More than anything, we want students to actually enjoy reading and to see it as a means to satisfy their curiosity about the world around them. Recent research has shown that students increase their reading skills and comprehension if they read out loud.

I would like to invite you to help me help your child become a better reader. It's simple. All you have to do is help your child with one short homework assignment each week. That's it!

Each _____ your child will have a short reading homework assignment that asks you to listen to him or her **read out loud** and answer a few easy questions. Each reading assignment is specifically created to reinforce a reading standard, or benchmark, that has been taught in class. With each assignment, I will include a letter to you that explains the skill being addressed, to better help you help your child. This simple project has been shown to improve reading fluency and comprehension, and with your help, I feel that it can benefit every child in my class.

You will have all week to complete the assignment and your child will get credit for doing the work. Just sign at the top of the page, indicating that you did, indeed, listen to your child read out loud and help him or her with the questions.

Please contact me if you have any questions concerning this project. The first lesson is attached and is due back by _____ . Thanks for all of your assistance in helping your child become the very best student he or she can be!

Sincerely,

Your child's teacher

Chapter 1

Fiction: Folk Tales, Fables, and Realistic Fiction

Passage	Skill	Standard
The Three Billy Goats Gruff	Determining the main idea; identifying supporting details	Determines main idea; identifies supporting details
The Fire on the Mountain	Recognizing compare and contrast	Recognizes the use of compare and contrast
The Grasshopper and the Ant	Identifying the theme in fiction	Uses literary terms
The Real Princess	Identifying story elements: conflict and resolution	Draws conclusions from story elements
The Man With the Coconuts	Identifying cause and effect	Recognizes cause-and-effect relationships
The Little Red Hen	Recognizing compare and contrast	Recognizes the use of compare and contrast
How the Camel Got His Hump	Identifying story elements: conflict and resolution	Draws conclusions from story elements
The Story of Snuggles	Understanding implied chronological order	Arranges events in chronological order
Michael's Racetrack	Making predictions; noticing irony	Makes predictions; uses literary terms

Many of the first seven stories in this chapter are familiar to teachers at every grade level. These tales and fables are retold here so that early readers can tackle them independently and still comprehend the main idea of each one. Make sure that your students are beginning to understand the differences among various genres, such as between the folk tales and the realistic fiction presented here. Even though this knowledge will not be tested until students are older, it is never too early to start using correct terms when discussing literature.

Week-by-Week Homework for Building Reading Comprehension and Fluency: Grades 2–3
SCHOLASTIC TEACHING RESOURCES

One of the activities in this chapter instructs students to draw a picture, in addition to responding with written answers. This technique offers a nice supplement for students and is an effective way to gauge their comprehension.

You can also have your students draw in response to stories read aloud in class. This activity challenges them to form images and perceptions from a listening experience. These drawings make great bulletin board displays, offering a springboard for discussing both the details in the stories and the students' own creative thinking.

The Three Billy Goats Gruff

Skill Focus: Determining the Main Idea; Identifying Supporting Details

To help your students understand the difference between the main idea and supporting details in a story, try retelling the story on a sheet of chart paper. List all of the events in order. Then challenge the class to tell the story using just three sentences. Number those three main events with 1, 2, and 3. Everything else is a supporting detail. This technique works with just about any primary-grade story.

Remember that on standardized tests, questions about main idea can make up as much as 40 percent of the test. That is one of the reasons you will see this skill focus repeated throughout this book.

Related Lessons

See additional lessons on Determining the Main Idea and Identifying Supporting Details in "Danger Ahead: The American Alligator" on page 43, and "Wham-O Toys" on page 70.

The Fire on the Mountain

Skill Focus: Recognizing Compare and Contrast

Learning to compare and contrast characteristics and elements is an important reading skill that is useful with both fiction and nonfiction reading passages. Its application is very basic and straightforward in this story. Introducing this complex skill at an early age gives students a good foundation on which to build in later years when they encounter more advanced passages.

Related Lessons

See additional lessons on Recognizing Compare and Contrast in "The Little Red Hen" on page 26, "Puzzled by Puzzles?" on page 68, and "Spaghetti Poems" on page 90.

The Grasshopper and the Ant

Skill Focus: Identifying the Theme in Fiction

There may well be disagreement among students, or between you and your students, about the lessons in this old tale. For instance, many children will say that the ant should have shared his food with the hungry grasshopper. You can debate these issues as much as you feel is appropriate for your students.

The underlying moral of this story, however, is that we should work hard and prepare for the future. That is the reason that the fable was written. Good readers need to be able to pick out the message intended by the author, whether they agree with it or not. To help students see this more clearly, it is a good idea to focus on this intended lesson, or moral, *before* the class debates the wisdom of the ant's decision.

The Real Princess

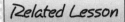 **Skill Focus:** Identifying Story Elements: Conflict and Resolution

Children need to learn about story elements and story line very early in their reading lives. The task in this assignment may seem quite simple, but it is a very important one. This lesson asks children to find three different elements of the story and mark them with crayons. Recognizing story elements in a simple story like this one facilitates other reading skills, such as sequencing. Moreover, it will prepare students for understanding story elements in the more complicated stories they will encounter later on.

Be sure to repeat this exercise in your classroom. To insure success, choose stories or articles for which the answers to your questions are clear and obvious.

Related Lesson

See additional lesson on Identifying Story Elements: Conflict and Resolution in "How the Camel Got His Hump" on page 28.

The Man With the Coconuts

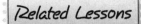 **Skill Focus:** Identifying Cause and Effect

Learning to recognize cause and effect is always difficult for students. This simple story is retold in a way that should help young readers grasp the cause-and-effect relationships and connections relatively easily. Be sure to point out additional examples of cause and effect on an ongoing basis, as you read other fiction and nonfiction stories in your classroom. Remember that virtually all standardized tests expect students to recognize when the author has used cause and effect in writing.

Related Lesson

See additional lesson on Identifying Cause and Effect in "Butch O'Hare" on page 52.

The Little Red Hen

 **Skill Focus:** Recognizing Compare and Contrast

This compare and contrast activity is a bit easier than the one that accompanies "The Fire on the Mountain" (see page 13). You may want to do this one first or reserve it for younger or struggling students. Remember that in compare and contrast questions, readers themselves are *not* the ones making the comparisons. Rather, students are expected to recognize when and how the author has used this literary convention. This concept may take some time for young students to understand.

Related Lessons

See additional lessons on Recognizing Compare and Contrast in "The Fire on the Mountain" on page 18, "Puzzled by Puzzles?" on page 68, and "Spaghetti Poems" on page 90.

How the Camel Got His Hump

Skill Focus: Identifying Story Elements: Conflict and Resolution

While identifying the central conflict and its resolution in a simple story like this may seem obvious to adults, it is sometimes quite tricky for young readers to be able to sort out these story elements. Because verbalizing concepts can help clarify and deepen their understanding, it is particularly important to have students state a story's conflict and resolution in their own words. By doing this simple exercise, students clarify events in their mind, focus on the main idea of the story, and verbalize what they have just learned. Using their own words to retell events builds a firm foundation for future reading comprehension.

The Story of Snuggles

Skill Focus: Understanding Implied Chronological Order

Children tend to remember the things that are most important to them, not necessarily the order in which they occurred. Thus, this apparently simple, basic skill of recognizing chronological order is not as easy as it seems. Help your students with this skill by asking them to orally retell events in a story. As they recall what happened, record the events on chart paper. Put the sentences in the correct order and leave spaces between the sentences to fill in gaps students may have omitted. When the chart is finished, the completed story will reflect correct chronological order, even if the students did not actually recall the events in the order in which they occurred. You can then use the chart to review the events and to help the students understand where their thinking or memory might have gotten off track. This activity works well with the whole class, after a class read-aloud, or alternately, with individual students who may need the extra reinforcement.

Michael's Racetrack

Skill Focus: Making Predictions; Noticing Irony

Primary-grade teachers often ask students to make predictions before they read a story. Predictions made before reading are typically based on prior knowledge about at topic, a study of the illustrations, or clues from the story's title. Predictions, however, can be made at any point *during* reading, as well. In this activity, there is a key prediction readers (both the children and their parents) are expected to make as they read the story.

It may seem a little early to introduce the concept of irony to students, but in this story, the irony should be quite accessible because it is central to the story's humorous twist. Students should be able to identify this twist at the end as what makes the story amusing, even if they don't quite grasp the full sense of irony. The little boy in the story appears to be doing everything that is expected of him, but instead all along he has a plan of his own. Even the most inexperienced readers in your class will understand and enjoy the surprise ending.

The Three Billy Goats Gruff

LISTEN to your child read this story aloud.

Once upon a time there were Three Billy Goats Gruff. One day they decided to cross a bridge and eat some new grass. But there was danger! Under the bridge lived a mean, ugly troll.

Trip, trap, trip, trap, went the Littlest Billy Goat as he walked on the bridge. "Who's that crossing over my bridge?" roared the troll.

"It is only I, the Littlest Billy Goat. I want to go to the hillside to eat the new grass."

"I'm going to gobble you up!" screamed the troll.

"I am so very little. Wait for my brother and you will get more to eat!"

"Okay. Be off with you then," said the troll.

Trip, trap, trip, trap, went the Middle-Sized Billy Goat as he walked on the bridge.

"Who's that crossing over my bridge?" roared the troll.

"It is only I, the Middle-Sized Billy Goat. I want to go to the hillside to eat the new grass."

"I'm going to gobble you up!" screamed the troll.

"Oh, don't eat me!" answered the Middle-Sized Billy Goat. "Wait for my biggest brother and you will get more to eat!"

"Okay. Be off with you then," said the troll.

TRIP, TRAP, TRIP, TRAP, went the Biggest Billy Goat as he walked on the bridge.

"Who's that crossing over my bridge?" roared the troll.

"It is I, the Biggest Billy Goat. I want to go to the hillside to eat the new grass."

"I'm going to gobble you up!" screamed the troll.

"You can't eat me! I am the Biggest Billy Goat." He lowered his head, stomped his feet, shook his horns, and charged at the troll. With one butt of his head he knocked the troll back in the water under the bridge.

And the third Billy Goat joined his brothers on the hillside to eat the new grass.

Retold by Mary Rose

Week-by-Week Homework for Building Reading Comprehension and Fluency: Grades 2–3
SCHOLASTIC TEACHING RESOURCES

Dear Parents,

Quite often teachers, as well as standardized tests, ask students to tell the difference between the main idea of a story and the supporting details. This is an important reading comprehension skill because it helps the reader to home in on major and minor concepts and to sort out the meaning of a story. In this story, the main idea is quite simple: the Three Billy Goats Gruff want to eat grass and the troll wants to eat them! Help your child understand this main message. All of the other information in the story is supporting detail.

We completed this assignment together.

_____

(Child's Signature)

_____

(Parent's Signature)

The Questions

The main idea of this story is that the Three Billy Goats Gruff want to eat grass and the troll wants to eat all of them. Everything else is a detail. Write five different details from the story of the Three Billy Goats Gruff.

1. _____

2. _____

3. _____

4. _____

5. _____

The Fire on the Mountain

LISTEN to your child read this story aloud.

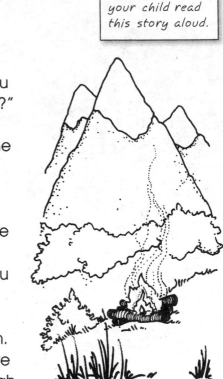

In the city of Addis Ababa lived Haptom Hasei. He was so rich that he was often bored. One night he called his servant, Arha. "How much cold can a man stand?" asked Haptom. "Can a man stand all night on the highest mountain in the coldest wind without a blanket or fire and not die?"

"I don't know," said Arha, "but wouldn't that be very foolish?"

"Perhaps, but what if there was a prize for doing it?"

"I am sure a brave man could do this, but I won't bet against you since I am a servant and I have nothing to bet."

"Well, I'll bet with you anyway. If you can stand among the rocks for an entire night without food or water or blankets or fire and not die, I will give you ten acres of farmland with a house and cattle."

Arha was so excited he agreed. The next morning he went to see Hailu, the wisest man he knew. Hailu said, "Tonight when you go to the mountain, I will build a fire here in the valley. All night long stare at it and think of its warmth. Your thoughts will keep you warm."

So that night Arha went to the top of the mountain. The servants of Haptom watched him to make sure he did not cheat. It was bitter cold and Arha was miserable. All night long he stood and stared at the fire in the valley.

The next morning he went to see Haptom. "You are a strong fellow," said Haptom. "How did you do this thing?"

"I looked at a fire in the valley," said Arha. "Thinking of the fire made me warm."

"Then you have cheated," said Haptom. "You used fire to live through the night. I will not give you the land."

Arha was very sad. He went to see Hailu, who promised to help his friend. Hailu held a feast at his house. He invited Haptom. It was a grand party, but Hailu would not serve the food. "Hailu, we are hungry. Why do you not feed us?" asked Haptom.

"Can you smell the food?" asked Hailu.

"Yes, we can smell it, but that smell does not make us full."

"It is the same as the distant fire that you can see, but not feel. If Arha was warmed by the fire in the valley, then you are fed by the smell of my food."

The people of the party all agreed. Haptom was ashamed and he gave the house, the cattle, and the ten acres of land to Arha.

Rewritten by Mary Rose
(Originally from *The Fire on the Mountain* by Harold Courlander and Wolf Leslau)

Dear Parents,

An important reading skill is that of comparing and contrasting elements within a given text. There are two different ways that a reader is expected to compare and contrast. Sometimes, we ask students to go beyond the text and to make comparisons based on their own life experiences. But most state assessments focus on another version of this skill. These tests do not ask the child to make comparisons from his or her own background knowledge. Instead, they expect the child to recognize when the author has used compare and contrast in a piece of writing. Both forms of the skill are valuable. In this assignment we focus on the kinds of comparisons that are built into a text by the author.

The Questions

Together write simple answers to the following questions.

Comparing Characters:

1. How are Haptom and Arha different at the beginning of the story?

_____

2. How are Haptom and Arha the same at the end of the story?

_____

Comparing Settings:

3. What is the setting in which Arha has to pass a test?

_____

4. What is the setting in which Haptom has to pass a test?

_____

Comparing Events:

5. What happens the night that Arha is being tested?

_____

6. What happens the night that Haptom is being tested?

_____

The Grasshopper and the Ant

LISTEN to your child read this story aloud.

Once there was a happy grasshopper. All summer long he hopped and leaped in the grass and lay in the warm sun. He was happy to be alive and spent every day doing all of the things he wanted to do. He ate the green grass and the leaves of the bushes. He sang his grasshopper songs and played in the summer rain. He slept under the roses and calmly watched all the other insects.

Living nearby was an ant. The ant was happy too, but she knew that summer would not last. The ant knew that soon the warm sun would be gone and winter would come. She dragged dead bugs into her nest. She stored little seeds to eat. She dug her home deep into the earth so she would not be cold later. She worked very hard all summer. She did not have time to sing and play.

The warm days of summer passed quickly. Soon all of the plants were dead and brown. All of the leaves had fallen to the ground. The sun was hidden behind clouds and the air was cold. The grasshopper was very hungry. He looked everywhere for something to eat, but couldn't find anything.

Then he saw the ant. "Please, Ant, will you give me something to eat?"

"Why should I give you something to eat? What have you been doing all summer while I worked to get ready for the cold?"

"I did not have time to work," said the grasshopper. "I sang songs, I hopped and leaped, and sat in the sun."

"Grasshopper, you played and never worked. I worked and never played. Why should I help you out when you did not help yourself?"

The grasshopper hopped slowly away and the ant went into her warm nest to nibble some seeds. "Foolish grasshopper," she said. "Now he will have to pay for the time he wasted. The winter will not be kind to the lazy one."

Retold by Mary Rose

Dear Parents,

This story is a fable. Not only does the story have talking animals, but they are there to teach us a lesson. In this story the animals don't say outright, "Be sure to work hard and save up for bad times." Instead, they give us the message implicitly, by showing us what happens to the poor grasshopper. We are supposed to imagine that something like this might happen to us and we are expected to learn from his mistakes. It is important for a reader to be able to figure out, or infer, the intended message of a reading passage. So this is one goal of the questions for this assignment. After you and your child answer the first three questions, discuss the lesson learned as you answer the final question.

We completed this assignment together.

_____
(Child's Signature)

_____
(Parent's Signature)

The Questions

✳ • ✳

Together write simple answers to the following questions.

1. What did the ant do all summer? _____

_____

_____

2. What did the grasshopper do all summer?

_____

_____

3. What happened when winter came?

_____

_____

4. What lesson did you learn from this story about the ant and the grasshopper?

_____

_____

The Real Princess

LISTEN to your child read this story aloud.

Once upon a time there was a prince who was looking for a real princess to marry. He looked and looked and looked. He wanted a real princess to be his wife. All of the girls he met had something wrong with them, and he knew they weren't really princesses.

One night there was a terrible storm. The wind blew and the rain came down very hard. Then there was a knock at the castle door. The king opened the door and saw a girl. She looked terrible. Her hair and clothes were wet and dirty, but she was very pretty.

The king let the girl come in the house. The queen said she could stay all night because of the storm. The girl said that she was a real princess. The queen decided to find out if this was true.

The queen put one single pea on the girl's bed. Then she placed twenty mattresses on top of the pea, and the girl went to sleep.

The next morning the king and queen asked the girl if she had a good night's sleep. She said no. She said that there was something hard in her bed and now she was black and blue.

The prince and the king and the queen knew that only a real princess could feel the pea through twenty mattresses. The prince married the princess and they lived happily ever after.

By Hans Christian Andersen. Retold by Mary Rose

Dear Parents,

In this lesson, children are trying to understand how the author develops a conflict, or problem, in a story and then solves it for the reader. Your child will be expected to do this with far more complicated plots in later grades, but we can begin building a foundation for this skill by starting with this simple story. Help your child identify the three major elements, or components, of this story: the problem, the solution, and the resolution.

1. What is the problem? (The prince wants a real princess.)
2. How does he solve the problem? (His mother uses a pea to determine if this is indeed a real princess.)
3. How is the problem resolved? (The pea test proves that she is a real princess and the prince marries her.)

Skill

Identifying Story Elements:
Conflict and Resolution

We completed this assignment together.

_____
(Child's Signature)

_____
(Parent's Signature)

The Questions

Get out your crayons or colored pencils. Go back to the first paragraph and draw a **red** circle around the one sentence that tells us the prince's problem. Go to the fourth paragraph and draw a **blue** circle around the words that describe what the queen did to solve the prince's problem. Use a **green** crayon to circle one sentence that tells how the story ends.

Now draw a picture of the princess and her bed with the pea and twenty mattresses on it. Ask your parent to help you count the mattresses correctly.

The Man With the Coconuts

LISTEN to your child read this story aloud.

One day a man went out to gather coconuts. He found a great many, so he put a heavy load of them on his horse and started home.

On the way he met a boy. The man said, "How long will it take me to reach my house?"

The boy looked at the heavy load of coconuts on the horse. Then he said, <u>"If you go slowly, you will arrive very soon, but if you go fast, it will take you all day to reach your house."</u>

The man thought over this strange speech, but he could not believe the boy. So he began to hurry his horse. The coconuts fell off, and he had to stop to pick them up.

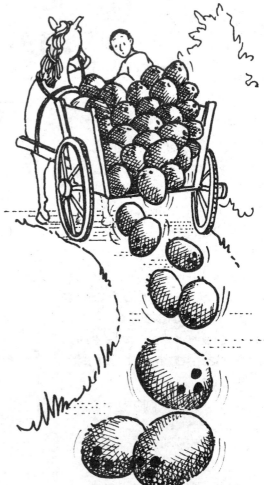

Then the man hurried his horse all the more to make up for the lost time. Again the coconuts fell off. Again the man had to stop and pick them all up.

Then he hurried his horse more than ever to make up for more lost time. Again and again the coconuts fell off. Again and again the man had to stop to pick them up. Again and again he hurried his horse more and more to make up for all of the time he had lost.

When at last he reached home, it was night. He thought of the boy's speech, but it did not seem strange to him anymore.

By Mabel Cook Cole

Week-by-Week Homework for Building Reading Comprehension and Fluency: Grades 2–3
SCHOLASTIC TEACHING RESOURCES

Dear Parents,

As with all these homework assignments, your child is supposed to read this story out loud to you. Because this is such an important aspect of these homework lessons, this letter focuses on a critical aspect of your child's reading and of your listening. While your child is reading, if you hear him or her make an error, do not rush to immediately point it out. Most of the time children themselves will hear an error and self-correct. If we correct children too quickly, they will learn to depend on us rather than learning to listen to themselves to insure that what they are reading makes sense.

The skill for this lesson is recognizing cause and effect.

We completed this assignment together.

_____
(Child's Signature)

_____
(Parent's Signature)

The Questions

Look carefully at what the little boy said. (The sentence is underlined in the story.) When we first read it, his sentence does not make sense. Later, it does. Write the answers to these questions to help you figure out why.

1. What was the cause of the man's problem? _____

_____

2. What was the effect of moving the horse faster? _____

_____

3. How did he try to solve the problem? _____

_____

4. Why was the little boy's sentence true? _____

_____

_____

The Little Red Hen

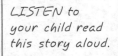
LISTEN to your child read this story aloud.

Once upon a time there was a little red hen who loved bread, so she wanted to plant wheat.

"Who will help me plant the wheat?" asked the little red hen.

"Not I," said the dog.

"Not I," said the cat.

"Not I," said the pig.

"Then I will do it myself," said the little red hen. And she did.

Soon the wheat was ready to cut. "Who will help me cut the wheat?" asked the little red hen.

"Not I," said the dog.

"Not I," said the cat.

"Not I," said the pig.

'Then I will do it myself," said the little red hen. And she did.

The wheat had to go to the mill to be ground into flour. "Who will help me take the wheat to the mill?" asked the little red hen.

"Not I," said the dog.

"Not I," said the cat.

"Not I," said the pig.

"Then I will do it myself," said the little red hen. And she did.

"Who will help me bake my bread?" asked the little red hen.

"Not I," said the dog.

"Not I," said the cat.

"Not I," said the pig.

"Then I will do it myself," said the little red hen. And the little red hen made bread.

When the bread was done, the little red hen asked, "Who will help me eat the bread?"

"I will," said the dog.

"I will," said the cat.

"I will," said the pig.

"No, you will not," said the little red hen. "You did not help me plant or cut or bake the bread. You will not help me eat it. I will eat it myself." And she did.

Retold by Mary Rose

Dear Parents,

In this familiar story, readers are again asked to make a comparison, this time between the little red hen and her friends, the dog, the cat, and the pig. Students will need to figure out how the little red hen is like her friends and how she is different from her friends. It is obvious to us that the little red hen is industrious and willing to work for what she gets, while her friends are lazy and want something for nothing. To help your child discover how the animals are alike, have him or her look at the first sentence of the story and then at how the animals respond to the freshly baked bread near the story's end.

As with other fables, your child should recognize that he or she is supposed to learn a lesson from the story. The final question focuses on this lesson and is intended to help your child articulate the underlying message.

We completed this assignment together.

_____

(Child's Signature)

_____

(Parent's Signature)

The Questions

Together write simple answers to the following questions.

1. Explain one way the little red hen is different from her friends. _____

_____

2. Explain one way the little red hen is like her friends. _____

_____

3. What lesson did you learn from the little red hen? _____

_____

How the Camel Got His Hump

LISTEN to your child read this story aloud.

Back when the world was new, animals began to do work for people. The horse with a saddle on his back came to the camel and said, "Oh, Camel, come and work like the rest of us."

But the camel did not want to work for people. He just said, "Humph!"

The dog with a stick in his mouth came to the camel and said, "Oh, Camel, come and fetch like the rest of us."

But the camel did not want to fetch. He just said, "Humph!"

Then the ox wearing a yoke on his neck came to the camel and said, "Oh, Camel, come and plow like the rest of us."

The camel did not want to plow. He just said, "Humph!"

This made the three animals very angry, so they went to talk to the Djinn in charge of all the deserts.*

The animals asked the Djinn, "Do you think it is fair that we have to work and the camel does not?"

"I do not think it is fair," said the Djinn. "I will teach Camel a lesson."

The Djinn went to the camel and asked him to help with the people's work.

But Camel just said, "Humph!"

"Since you just keep saying 'Humph!' I will give you a 'humph'," said the Djinn.

Then the camel's back began to swell up to a big hump.

"Now you are going to work for people," said the Djinn. "You will walk in the desert for days and live from the water and food in your hump."

And so the camel learned how to work, but he has never learned how to be polite when people are around.

* In Muslim legend, a Djinn is a supernatural figure who affects the lives of men and women.

By Rudyard Kipling. Retold by Mary Rose

Dear Parents,

Understanding plot development and conflict resolution may sound like very sophisticated skills for elementary school students, but even young children can learn these concepts if they are presented in the context of simple text with a simple story line. Most stories follow a pattern. The story begins with a problem that needs to be resolved. Certain actions happen in the middle, and the ending solves the original problem. This pattern is true of simple stories and even of much of the world's great literature. This homework assignment asks students to define the main conflict in a story and to determine how it is resolved. Please help your child complete this page using his or her own words.

We completed this assignment together.

_____
(Child's Signature)

_____
(Parent's Signature)

The Questions

Together write simple answers to the following questions.

1. What is the main problem in this story? _____

_____

2. How did the Djinn help the animals solve their problem? _____

_____

3. What lesson did the camel learn from the Djinn and the animals? _____

_____

The Story of Snuggles

LISTEN to your child read this story aloud.

Suddenly everything was quiet. The tiny dog blinked her big brown eyes, but she couldn't see any anything. She began to whimper, but no humans came to help her. She wagged her tail, but no hands came to pet her. She sniffed the air, but could not smell anything that reminded her of home. She was hungry and cold. She began to walk in the rain.

In the morning she saw that she was in a street, but it was not her street. She walked up to a man, but he kept going. She saw some children go by on bikes. Then a soft voice said, "Where are you going, little one? Have you been out here all night?"

A lady took the tired, wet dog home. She rubbed her dry and gave her some food, but the little dog was still shaking and afraid and stayed by herself. For one whole week the lady tried to find the owner of the dog. One day Lana, a little girl from next door, came to visit. She sat on the floor and the little dog crawled into her lap and went to sleep.

"You may have her," said the lady, "but she is still very scared of everything. I think she was blown away from her family in the big tornado we had here last week."

"She is shaking," said Lana. "And look how she hides her head in my arms."

"This little dog will need lots of love to make her forget a tornado," the lady told Lana.

"I will name her Snuggles! Every time she is scared, she can snuggle with me."

Snuggles whimpered and wagged her tail and Lana smiled. The tiny dog had found a new home at last.

By Mary Rose

Dear Parents,

Life may happen chronologically, but literature does not have to! In more advanced reading, students will discover flashbacks and time shifts that are often quite subtle. Even in beginning short stories like this one, the order of events may not be clear. In this story about Snuggles, your child may not realize the correct order of events because the occurrence of a tornado is not revealed until the last part of the story. Because readers need to put pieces together themselves, this is called implied chronological order. It is more difficult to recognize than straightforward time order in which events are clearly told in sequence.

Skill

Understanding Implied
Chronological Order

We completed this
assignment together.

_____
(Child's Signature)

_____
(Parent's Signature)

The Questions

Together write simple answers to the following questions.

1. What event happened first?
(**Hint:** Be careful! It is not what the story describes first!) _____

_____

2. What happened second in the story? _____

_____

3. What happened last in the story? _____

_____

Michael's Racetrack

LISTEN to your child read this story aloud.

For two weeks, five-year-old Michael kept asking his parents to let him drive his new race car. Every morning and every night he would say, "Please, Mommy, please. I need to drive my cars."

Michael's father built a racing track in the backyard that was just the right size for the new car. Then one evening after supper, Michael's father helped him put on his racing clothes. He had a tiny racing suit that zipped up the front. He had a racing helmet. He had racing gloves and shoes. He even had goggles. His father strapped him safely into the car and started the engine.

Michael's mother got out some chairs and iced tea. She put the chairs near the big track in the backyard. She sat down and waited to watch Michael drive his car round and round the track.

Here came Michael! But then he did something his mother didn't expect. He drove off the racetrack and onto the grass in the middle of the track. He turned the steering wheel all the way to the left and shoved the gas pedal down hard. The car began to spin in a circle. Three times around he went.

The tires made a perfect circle of dirt in the grass. Then Michael turned off the car and climbed out. He seemed to know just what he wanted. He sat on the ground and reached into his pocket. He got out his favorite tiny toy cars and began to play with them in the new flattened dirt.

Michael's parents looked at each other and burst out laughing. They realized now that Michael had not really wanted to drive his big race car. Instead, he had his own plan. He had just needed to make a perfect, little racetrack for his toy cars.

By Susan Seay

Week-by-Week Homework for Building Reading Comprehension and Fluency: Grades 2–3
SCHOLASTIC TEACHING RESOURCES

Dear Parents,

This story has been included because it has a surprise ending. The whole story builds up to the main event of Michael's driving his race car around the track, but in the end, he doesn't drive it around the track at all.

It is important to encourage children to make predictions, both before and during reading, about what they think will happen in the story. It is equally important to check later to see if the predictions turned out to be correct.

When the story has an unusual twist, as this one does, it is called "irony." While we do not expect young students to grasp the concept of irony, they can certainly see the humor in this situation. In later reading, they will be able to connect the idea of irony with the humorous or, at least as often, tragic results that such unexpected twists typically bring to a plot.

Skill
Making Predictions; Noticing Irony

We completed this assignment together.

_____

(Child's Signature)

_____

(Parent's Signature)

The Questions

✳ • ✳

Together write simple answers to the following questions.

1. What did Michael's parents expect him to do with his real race car?

_____

2. Did you expect the same thing? _____

3. Michael did not do what everyone thought he would. What did he do instead?

_____

4. Michael gave a tiny hint about his plan when he kept asking to drive. What did he say to his mother that might be a clue?

_____

5. How did Michael's parents feel about what he did? _____

How do you know? _____

Chapter 2

Animals and Nature

Passage	Skill	Standard
John Silver the Pigeon	Separating root words and suffixes	Recognizes root words, suffixes, etc.
The American Bald Eagle	Distinguishing fact from opinion	Recognizes differences in fact and opinion
Know About Snow?	Identifying the theme in nonfiction	Uses literary terms
Danger Ahead: The American Alligator	Determining the main idea; identifying supporting details	Determines main idea; identifies relevant supporting details
Hoffman's Sloth	Identifying the author's purpose	Identifies author's purpose

sually children enjoy learning about animals and nature, but most of their learning has come secondhand, from an adult reading to them or from something they have watched on television. This chapter provides students with an opportunity to begin getting information on their own. They usually feel very grown up when they can read nonfiction books and articles independently.

Try to provide your students with additional nonfiction books that will supplement their knowledge of animals and nature. If time allows, try comparing the animals in those books with the animals in these articles. For instance, match books about rain or fog to the article about snow. Use your own materials as pre-teaching resources or as follow-up to the lessons in this chapter.

John Silver the Pigeon

Skill Focus: Separating Root Words and Suffixes

Teach students to use their knowledge of affixes (prefixes and suffixes) to help with reading, word meanings, and spelling. Students should understand that the addition of the suffix *-ed* to a verb indicates that an action has already happened and has been completed. The suffix *-ly* is added to create an adverb, which describes *how* something looked, felt, acted, and so on. The suffix *-ing* affects the meaning and function of a word in different ways. When added to a verb, it indicates that an action is progressing or continuing to happen. It can also change a verb to an adjective, called a *participle*, as in John Silver's own identity—"homing pigeon."

The American Bald Eagle

Skill Focus: Distinguishing Fact From Opinion

Even older students have difficulty separating fact from opinion. Give your students practice by discussing this page together as a class after they have returned the assignment to you for grading. You may wind up with some classroom debate, but with your guidance this can be a helpful means for students to clarify the distinctions. You might tell your students that one way to figure out if a statement is an opinion is to ask yourself, "Would this sentence appear in a nonfiction textbook?" If not, it is probably an opinion.

Know About Snow?

Skill Focus: Identifying the Theme in Nonfiction

Primary-grade teachers often ask students to identify themes in fiction, but national standards, or benchmarks, require them to be able to identify themes in nonfiction as well. This is usually quite a difficult task for young children. Practicing with this easy article about snow should help them begin to grasp the concept of theme.

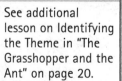

Related Lesson

See additional lesson on Identifying the Theme in "The Grasshopper and the Ant" on page 20.

    In this piece, you will notice that each paragraph focuses on certain facts about snow. These facts make up the main idea: snow is wonderful and amazing, manifested in different varieties and uniquely shaped flakes. However, the skill for this lesson is "identifying the theme in nonfiction." The theme is a less definite message than the main idea. It is conveyed in every paragraph, differing only slightly but nonetheless significantly from the main idea. The theme of this article would be the author's multi-leveled fascination with snow. Remember to ask students about themes as you read other nonfiction texts.

Danger Ahead: The American Alligator

Skill Focus: Determining the Main Idea; Identifying Supporting Details

The primary objective of this activity is to help students identify the main idea in a nonfiction text passage. But the activity goes further than that. After the students have identified the main idea, they are asked to list the supporting details. On standardized tests, students often have to demonstrate that they can separate the main idea from the supporting sentences. This lesson provides good practice for learning this skill.

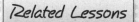

Related Lessons

See additional lessons on Determining the Main Idea; Identifying Supporting Details in "The Three Billy Goats Gruff" on page 16, and "Wham-O Toys" on page 70.

Hoffman's Sloth

Skill Focus: Identifying the Author's Purpose

Questions that ask students to identify the author's purpose are among the most frequently missed on state assessments. Be sure to share the PIE (Persuade, Inform, or Entertain) acronym with children, perhaps by displaying it in your classroom on a large chart. And remember to refer to it often during everyday classroom reading, asking students on a regular basis to identify the author's purpose in just about anything the class or an individual is reading.

As students get older, it's important for teachers to connect different kinds of writing assignments with the three major categories of author's purposes. If you ask your students to make up and write a narrative story, the underlying purpose will likely be to *entertain* the audience. If you assign them a science report, the purpose will be to *inform* readers about the science project. The third purpose is *persuasion*. We rarely ask students to write persuasively until the fifth or sixth grade, but even young children may be able to identify examples of persuasion in television commercials, especially those selling breakfast cereal or toys.

John Silver the Pigeon

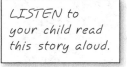
LISTEN to your child read this story aloud.

When you walk down any city street, you will see birds called pigeons. There are many kinds of pigeons, and one special kind is called the "homing pigeon." Homing pigeons were used before there were radios or telephones. These birds are especially smart. When they are taken to places far from their homes and released, these pigeons actually fly straight back home.

During World War I, the army found these birds to be very useful. A soldier would put a little silver tube on a pigeon's leg and place an important message inside. He would then let the bird go and it would fly home, where another soldier was waiting to receive the note. These birds were a great help to the soldiers.

One homing pigeon was released during a battle at Meuse-Argonne in France in World War I. An explosion near the pigeon tossed him around, but he kept flying. When he finally got back to his home, he was almost dead. Part of his chest was gone and his right leg was missing, but the message tube was still there.

The men named him "John Silver" after the one-legged pirate in Robert Louis Stevenson's *Treasure Island*. He was treated kindly and honored as a war hero.

At the Wright Patterson Air Museum in Dayton, Ohio, you can still see John Silver. He is on display with famous airplanes and artifacts from wars. Every year on an army holiday called Organization Day, they call out the names of soldiers who died in wars. When the name "John Silver" is called, a soldier always replies, "Died of wounds received in battle in the service of his country."

Who would have thought that a pigeon could be a war hero? The next time you see pigeons strutting on the sidewalk, think of the homing pigeon, John Silver.

By Mary Rose

Dear Parents,

One way to help children with unfamiliar words is to teach them to "take the word apart" and look for something that they recognize—a root word or an affix, which can be either a prefix or a suffix. A root word is the base word before anything is added. An affix is the part that gets added. Suffixes are groups of letters added to the end of a word. For example, if you start with the word official and add the suffix, -ly, you come up with a new word, officially. When children can identify root words and separate them from the suffixes, it helps them sound out and pronounce the word, and also helps them understand the word's meaning.

We completed this assignment together.

_____

(Child's Signature)

_____

(Parent's Signature)

The Questions

This week's story contains many examples of root words with suffixes. See if you can find the root word and suffix of these words. Then look carefully in the story to add even more to the list.

Word	Root Word	Suffix
kindly	_____	_____
useful	_____	_____
tossed	_____	_____
finally	_____	_____
named	_____	_____
strutting	_____	_____
_____	_____	_____
_____	_____	_____
_____	_____	_____

The American Bald Eagle

LISTEN to your child read this story aloud.

How much do you know about the symbol of America, the bald eagle? First of all, when we are talking about birds, *bald* does not mean "no hair on the head." A bird is bald if it has a white-feathered spot on its head. Both the eagle's head and its tail are white, and it has black feathers on the rest of its body. It is a beautiful bird.

The eagle is huge. If a grown man stretched out his arms as wide as they could go, he could not stretch them as wide as an eagle's wings. These wings can span seven and a half feet from the end of one wing to the end of the other. The eagle is amazing.

The eagle also has excellent vision. It can see things from far away, and that makes it a great hunter. It can see a fish even if the fish is underwater. That good vision means that the eagle is wonderful.

Each one of the eagle's claws can be over an inch long. Those claws, or *talons*, help it to catch its supper. They even have bumps on them to keep slippery fish from wiggling free. The eagle would probably be a very unhappy bird if it didn't have those claws.

The eagle also has a very sharp beak. The beak can be as long as two inches and is very strong. It could probably eat any fish it wanted in five minutes by using that beak.

You can find a picture of the eagle on coins and on the Great Seal of the United States of America. The bald eagle is the best bird in the country.

By Mary Rose

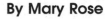

Dear Parents,

This lesson is intended to help your child tell the difference between facts and opinions, a very important skill in our world. This story appears to be factual, but it contains one opinion sentence in each paragraph. Help your child understand that a fact is something that can be proved. Ask your child if we can prove that a dog has four paws. How can we do this? An opinion is something that a person thinks or feels. It may or may not be true; there is no way it can be proved. People may disagree about opinions, but not about facts. Ask your child if we can prove that a dog is the best animal in the world. Why or why not? Discussions like this should help your child to see the difference between these two kinds of statements.

We completed this assignment together.

_____
(Child's Signature)

_____
(Parent's Signature)

The Questions

✳ • • • • • • • • • • • • • • • • ✳

Find an opinion sentence in each paragraph and write it here.

1. _____

_____

2. _____

_____

3. _____

_____

4. _____

_____

5. _____

_____

6. _____

_____

Know About Snow?

LISTEN to your child read this story aloud.

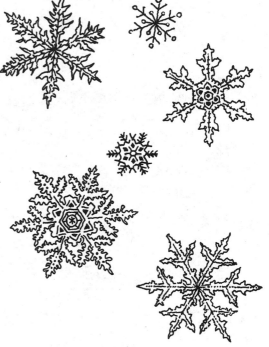

We love to roll in it, catch it on our tongues, play with it, throw it, ski and sled in it, make pretend ice cream out of it, and just look at its beauty. It is cold. It is white. It is wonderful. What is it? SNOW!

In 1931, Wilson Alwyn Bentley photographed snowflakes and published the pictures in a book called *Snow Crystals.* Before then, people had not realized that snowflakes were really crystals, and they did not know that every flake that ever fell from the sky was different from every other one.

The shape of a snow crystal depends on how cold the weather is, how much water is in the air, and how hard the wind is blowing. Snowflakes can look like stars, columns, plates, or bullets. Most often the crystals freeze together and make a six-pointed star. The shape of the crystals determines if the snowflakes will make a light and fluffy powder—which is great for skiing—or if it will make the thick and heavy snow that is perfect for making snowmen.

The next time you are in snow, do what Mr. Bentley did. Let a few flakes fall onto something that is dark colored, and use a small magnifying lens to look at them. You are sure to see beautiful snowflakes and you can remember, as you play in the snow, that each one is different.

By Mary Rose

Dear Parents,

We often ask children to find themes in short stories and in other fiction, but they also need to be able to identify themes in nonfiction material. This article on snow will give them an opportunity to do just that.

The theme is actually like the main idea, but it is not a direct summation of the facts. In this article, the author clearly states facts that provide specific answers to the questions below. These facts make up the main idea. But the theme goes one step beyond—it is the underlying message of all of these paragraphs put together. Ask your child (and yourself) how the author feels about snow. Look at each paragraph and see if something there proves you are correct. When you have decided what feeling or message is everywhere in the piece, you have identified the theme.

We completed this assignment together.

_____
(Child's Signature)

_____
(Parent's Signature)

The Questions

1. What is this article mainly about? (**Hint:** You need to write more than just one word here!)

_____

_____

2. What are two things you learned from reading this article?

_____

_____

3. What is the theme of this article?

_____

_____

Danger Ahead: The American Alligator

LISTEN to your child read this story aloud.

There are just two kinds of alligators in the world. One is the Chinese alligator, which lives in the Yangtze River in China. It is only about five feet long and is not dangerous to humans.

The other alligator is the American alligator. It can be as long as 20 feet, and it is *very* dangerous to humans. American alligators will eat almost anything that shows up near their watery homes. They can eat fish, frogs, snakes, turtles, birds, raccoons, dogs, and cats. They will attack humans, too. And just because an alligator *looks* like it is asleep, don't think that it really is. Don't go near it. When an American alligator decides to attack, it moves as fast as lightning—you cannot possibly run fast enough to escape!

Alligators have really strong jaws and large, sharp teeth. They can kill most animals with just one quick bite. If the bite doesn't kill the prey, the alligator will drag it underwater to drown it.

The most dangerous time to be around an alligator is in the spring when the female has babies. She lays her eggs in a nest of mud and plants and stays nearby to keep them safe. When the eggs hatch, she becomes a very gentle and protecting mother. To move her babies to a safe place, the mother alligator makes many trips, gently carrying baby alligators inside her huge mouth. She cares for them and leads them around for one whole year, until they can take care of themselves. She is such a protecting mother that she will do almost anything—and attack almost anything—to keep her babies safe.

So, unless you are in China or unless you are a baby alligator, stay away from these dangerous animals!

By Mary Rose

Dear Parents,

After a child reads a nonfiction article like this one about alligators, he or she should be able to describe what that article was about. Usually all we are looking for here is a one- or two-word or, at most, a one-sentence answer. When the child is able to give you "the gist" of the story in that concise way, he or she has identified the main idea. (**Hint:** The main idea is often suggested by the title of the piece.)

In this activity, we are also asking the child to identify the supporting details. These are the sentences that provide evidence for, or prove, the main idea. After your child has written the title and the main idea of the article, help him or her to find five things that tell how we know that alligators are dangerous. Those five things are supporting details because they supply the supporting evidence for the main idea.

We completed this assignment together.

_____

(Child's Signature)

_____

(Parent's Signature)

The Questions

❋ • ❋

1. What is the title of this article? _____

2. What is the main idea of this article? _____

_____

3. The author told about five things to make sure you understood the main idea. List at least three of them on the lines below.

_____

_____

_____

_____

Hoffman's Sloth

The Hoffman's sloth is one of the strangest animals in the world. First of all, the sloth hangs upside down in a tree almost its whole life. It also has very unusual fur. Take a look at a dog's fur. It grows from the dog's back and hangs down toward the belly. The sloth's fur grows in the opposite direction, from its belly to its back. So even though rain falls on this sloth about four or five times every day, the rainwater runs right off the sloth's fur.

There's something even more amazing about this sloth. There is a little line in each hair. Inside those lines grow tiny green plants called algae. There is so much algae living in the sloth's fur that it makes the whole animal look like a clump of green moss. The sloth is nearly invisible!

The Hoffman's sloth has three toes on its back feet, but only two claws on its hands. The claws are long and sharp and help the animal hang upside down for its whole life. The sloth can also fight with its claws.

Because sloths hang upside down so much, their back muscles are very weak, and they cannot walk. If they go to the ground to get to a new tree, they drag themselves along with their claws.

The sloth does *everything* upside down. It eats, sleeps, and has babies while it hangs in a tree. Most of the time it does nothing except eat leaves, fruits, and small twigs—and sleep! Now that you have read about the Hoffman's sloth, do you agree that it is very strange?

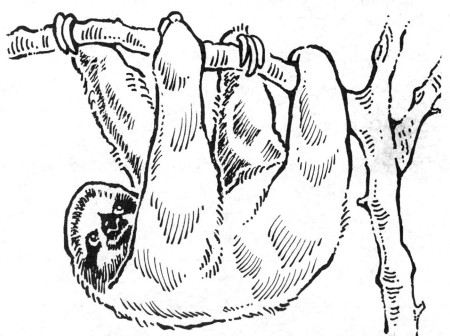

By Mary Rose

Dear Parents,

One kind of question frequently found on standardized tests asks students to determine the author's purpose in a certain piece of writing. The acronym PIE is an easy way to help your child remember the three main purposes an author might have. PIE stands for Persuade, Inform, or Entertain. Generally speaking, nonfiction writing, which typically explains facts, is aimed at informing readers. Poetry and narrative stories are usually geared toward entertaining. Editorials, advertisements, and certain essays try to persuade readers. Even young readers are expected to know these differences. In some states, students must not only identify the author's purpose, but they must also explain that purpose in their own words.

We completed this assignment together.

_____

(Child's Signature)

_____

(Parent's Signature)

The Questions

1. Circle the correct answer. What was the author's purpose for writing "Hoffman's Sloth"?

    A. <u>to persuade</u> us to like the sloth

    B. <u>to inform</u> us about the sloth

    C. <u>to tell a story</u> about the sloth

2. Tell at least two things that made you choose this answer.

_____

_____

_____

Bonus: Color the sloth on page 45. What color should it be? (**Hint:** The author *informed* you about the color.)

Famous People

Passage	Skill	Standard
Paul Revere	Recognizing appositives	Uses context clues
Butch O'Hare	Identifying cause and effect	Recognizes cause-and-effect relationships
Otis	Recognizing synonyms	Identifies synonyms in context
The General and the Corporal	Differentiating between past- and present-tense verbs	Recognizes parts of speech
Marco Polo	Using references; factual recall	Constructs meaning from reading selections

By the second and third grade, students are beginning to recognize the names of prominent people such as Abraham Lincoln and Martin Luther King, Jr. This chapter contains information about a few very famous people and some not-quite-so-famous people whom students would probably not read about elsewhere. It broadens young children's background knowledge of the world to be exposed to individuals from a variety of time periods and professions. We hope your students enjoy these interesting glimpses into the lives of people who have made a difference in our world.

This chapter provides you with the tools to introduce your students to some basic skills in literacy. Because it may be students' first experience with some of these skills, make sure you have taught them in class before sending home these homework pages. As with all the assignments in this book, the homework lessons are intended to be practice and reinforcement, not instruction. Teaching ahead insures, too, that homework assignments will not create frustration for the children or their parents.

Paul Revere

Skill Focus: Recognizing Appositives

The focus of this lesson is helping your students recognize appositives—words or phrases that rename a term that has come before. Recognizing appositives not only enhances readers' use of context clues, it also proves very valuable when students are asked comprehension questions on tests.

Point out that appositives do not only refer to people, but also to places or descriptions. Appositives can also refer to phrases, as well as single words. Look for appositives in all nonfiction texts, including science and social studies books. Pause when the class encounters an appositive and make sure that they recognize it. Even more important, make sure they understand the information the author is trying to convey and how the appositive helps in this process. Look for appositives in fiction, too. For example: Dorothy, and her three friends, the scarecrow, the tin man, and the cowardly lion, went to see the Wizard of Oz. In this sentence, "the scarecrow, the tin man, and the cowardly lion" forms the appositive that explains the words "three friends."

Butch O'Hare

Skill Focus: Identifying Cause and Effect

It is not very often that young children have an opportunity to read about a man as brave and well-respected as Butch O'Hare. In this activity, students are asked to focus on one of the more difficult reading skills (and standards, or benchmarks)—identifying the cause-and-effect text pattern. This story is specifically targeted to help young readers with this skill because the lines of cause and effect are clearly drawn.

> **Related Lesson**
>
> See additional lesson on Identifying Cause and Effect in "The Man With the Coconuts" on page 24.

Otis

Skill Focus: Recognizing Synonyms

This story contains numerous synonyms; thus in reading the passage, young readers will need to recognize and become familiar with them.

Remember to point out similarities in word meanings whenever you find them. Because many simple stories and articles for young readers do not contain synonyms on the same page or within the same chapter, you will need to make a point of comparing them across stories or academic areas.

The General and the Corporal

Skill Focus: Differentiating Between Past- and Present-Tense Verbs

Children often use correct verb tenses without even realizing that their spoken verbs are indicating different tenses: past, present, or future. They do this automatically, as part of normal language development. Because developing language users overgeneralize, second and third graders often have difficulty with irregular verbs such as *swim* and *run*. They tend to say *swimmed,* not *swam,* and *runned,* not *ran,* because that is the pattern a regular verb would follow. Such verbs do need to be taught, in targeted lessons on irregular verb formation. But, of course, students also need lessons like this one in order to help them explicitly recognize and understand regular verb endings that indicate tense.

Marco Polo

Skill Focus: Using References; Factual Recall

Many state standards, or benchmarks, for teaching literacy include a standard such as, "uses a variety of reference materials." This is a skill we should be teaching students even at grades two and three. You can begin introducing this skill with the simple activity in this lesson—having students trace a path on a map. This should be only among the first of many such activities you engage in with your students to give them practice working with texts and maps.

> **Related Lesson**
>
> See additional lesson on Factual Recall in "Old Mother Hubbard" on page 79.

Paul Revere

Have you ever heard of the midnight ride of Paul Revere? Well, the king of England ruled America at one time. But there were many people, called <u>patriots</u>, who did not like the king. They wanted this to be a separate country.

The king decided to send some soldiers to Boston to force the people to obey his laws. The patriots were in <u>Charlestown</u>, a town across the Charles River from Boston. They had gunpowder in <u>Concord</u>, another town 18 miles away. The British soldiers heard about the gunpowder and they decided to get it for themselves.

Paul Revere learned that the <u>regulars</u> (the king's soldiers from England) were going to Concord. He wanted to stop them. A friend told Paul Revere that he would watch to see when the British soldiers were coming and give Paul a signal. If they were on land, he would hang one lantern in the steeple of the Old North Church. If they were coming across the river, he would hang two lanterns.

When Paul saw two lights in the steeple, he knew the soldiers were coming across the river. He jumped on his horse and rode fast. He woke up the people by screaming, "The regulars are coming out!"

The patriots left their houses and went to fight against the <u>redcoats</u>, the British soldiers who were dressed in bright red uniforms. The British soldiers went on to Concord, but they did not get the gunpowder.

Everyone thanked Paul Revere for waking them to fight and save their homes from the British soldiers. Even today we talk about the bravery of the man who rode those famous 18 miles.

By Mary Rose

Dear Parents,

We can help improve students' understanding of written material by teaching them about appositives. Appositives are words or phrases that restate or add information. Read the following sentence: Chuck Yeager, <u>the first man to break the sound barrier</u>, is famous for helping to start the NASA space program. The underlined phrase is an appositive for "Chuck Yeager." The phrase adds information and tells us a little bit more about who Chuck Yeager is. Without instruction, children often read this kind of sentence without making the connection between "Chuck Yeager" and "the man who was the first to break the sound barrier." When students learn to recognize an appositive and to understand its relationship to the word or phrase that comes before it, their comprehension will greatly improve.

We completed this assignment together.

_____
(Child's Signature)

_____
(Parent's Signature)

The Questions

1. Look at the following list of words from this story. Go back to the text and find the phrase that comes right after each word. That phrase is an appositive. It helps you understand the meaning of the word. Write each appositive in the space provided.

   patriots _____

   Charlestown _____

   Concord _____

   regulars _____

   redcoats _____

2. Write one sentence of your own that contains an appositive. _____

   _____

   _____

Butch O'Hare

LISTEN to your child read this story aloud.

In World War II, many battles were fought by pilots of airplanes that took off from aircraft carriers in the Pacific Ocean. One of these American fighter pilots was named Butch O'Hare.

One day when he was in flight, he realized that he was running out of fuel. His commander told him to go back to the carrier alone. On his way back, he saw some Japanese Zeros (fighter planes) heading toward his ship. He thought of the thousands of men who would die if the Japanese bombs hit the carrier. He thought of his friends in the other airplanes who would have no place to land if the carrier was blown up.

So even though he was all alone, he attacked. He shot at the planes until all of his bullets were gone. Then he tried to fly into the other planes and destroy them. The Japanese fighters shot O'Hare's plane many times. But finally they gave up, and Butch landed his damaged plane on the aircraft carrier.

His plane had cameras that recorded everything he did. When people saw the films of his fight against so many enemy planes, they were amazed that he had not been killed, that his plane could still fly, and that he had risked his life to save the lives of the men on the ship.

After the war, Butch O'Hare was called a hero and was given medals for his bravery. Later, Chicago's airport was named after him. Today, O'Hare Airport is one of the busiest airports in the world, but very few people know that the airport is named for Butch O'Hare, a genuine American hero.

By Mary Rose

Week-by-Week Homework for Building Reading Comprehension and Fluency: Grades 2–3
SCHOLASTIC TEACHING RESOURCES

Dear Parents,

Young readers need to be able to determine cause and effect in fiction, nonfiction (like this true story), poetry, and even in drama. Help your child to understand these terms by using them in your daily conversations. For example, you might say, "You left your skateboard outside in the rain (cause) so now it is rusted" (effect). It is often easier for children to understand this concept if we begin with the effect. So try turning these statements around, too: "Your skateboard is rusted (effect) because you left it out in the rain" (cause).

We completed this assignment together.

_____

(Child's Signature)

_____

(Parent's Signature)

The Questions

❋ • ❋

1. What are some events in the story that show that Butch O'Hare was brave?

_____

2. Why did Butch O'Hare act so bravely? _____

_____

3. Name two good things that happened because Butch O'Hare was brave.

_____

_____

Otis

LISTEN to your child read this story aloud.

Do you know anyone named Otis? You have probably ridden in a machine that was one of Otis's inventions. Elisha Otis invented the safety elevator and started the Otis Elevator Company in 1853.

The word *elevator* comes from *elevate*, which means "to lift." In fact, in England, people call an elevator a "lift."

Even before Otis, there were elevators. The Greeks used ropes and pulleys to move things from one floor up to another. In ancient Rome, they built a special kind of elevator to move lions and gladiators up to the arenas. Miners used a different kind of elevator to move coal and ore out of mines. But these early elevators were unsafe. Before Otis invented the stopping device, safety brakes, it was dangerous for people to ride in elevators because if the ropes broke, the whole thing would crash to the bottom.

Otis made it so safe to ride an elevator that tall buildings could be built and people could ride to the top floors without danger. One of the first places to use an Otis elevator was the Eiffel Tower in Paris. It opened in 1889. Soon more tall buildings were erected. In New York City, the Woolworth Building was built in 1913 and the Empire State Building was built in 1931. Both of these towering structures used Otis elevators to convey people up and down the skyscrapers.

It all began in 1853, and we are still riding in very safe Otis elevators today!

By Mary Rose

Dear Parents,

This week's lesson focuses on synonyms. The article about the Otis Elevator Company was written with specific attention to synonyms—different words that have the same meaning. One way you can help your child understand synonyms is by using them in your everyday conversation. Here are two examples: "I hope you had a terrific time at the party. Was it really wonderful?" or "That meal was really tasty. I'd call it delicious."

We completed this assignment together.

_____
(Child's Signature)

_____
(Parent's Signature)

The Questions

Synonyms are words that have the same or almost the same meaning. Below is a list of words from the story about the Otis Elevator Company. Find another word in the story that is a synonym for the given word. Write it on the line.

1. elevate _____

2. started _____

3. unsafe _____

4. tall _____

5. built _____

6. ride _____

The General and the Corporal

LISTEN to your child read this story aloud.

You probably know about our first president, George Washington. Many people think of him as one of the greatest men in American history.

One winter day, while his army was building fences and cabins to make a camp in the winter, General Washington walked around to see how things were going. He walked past a man giving orders to the other men. The man giving the orders was a corporal, the lowest ranking officer in an army.

General Washington noticed that the men were struggling to lift a heavy log. The corporal shouted at the men to try harder to lift the log, but he never offered to help.

Finally, General Washington, who was very tall and strong, stepped in to help the men. Soon they lifted the log in place. He looked at the corporal and asked, "Why aren't you helping your men with this heavy lifting? "

"Why?" said the man. "I am a corporal! I am an important man."

"Oh, indeed," said Washington. "Well, I am the general, and the next time you have a log that is too heavy for your men to lift, send

for me." Then he unbuttoned his coat and showed the uniform that he was wearing.

The little corporal felt terrible when he saw that it was the great General George Washington who had helped with the work. He realized something important then. Truly great men are never too great to help others.

Retold by Mary Rose
(Originally from Baldwin's Readers, American Book Company © 1897)

Dear Parents,

This story is written in the past tense, because it describes events that took place many years ago. But there are three places in the story that are written in the present tense: the first paragraph, which is addressed directly to the reader in the present; the dialogue between the corporal and the general; and the final sentence, which states the story's lesson. Dialogue is always written in the present tense because it conveys the words of the speaker himself as he experiences events in a particular moment in time. The lesson, or moral of the story, is in the present tense because it not connected to a particular moment in time. Help your child to recognize the difference between past tense and present tense by choosing one of these examples and contrasting it with the rest of the story. It may help your child if he or she identifies and circles the -ed verbs first. Verbs ending in -ed always indicate past tense; thus, all the -ed words in this article occur within the historical story.

We completed this assignment together.

_____

(Child's Signature)

_____

(Parent's Signature)

The Questions

※ • ※

Verbs that end in -ed are in the past tense. List eight past tense verbs here.

_____   _____

_____   _____

_____   _____

_____   _____

Bonus: Can you find four verbs that are in the present tense? Write them here.

_____   _____

_____   _____

Marco Polo

What do you think of when you hear the name Marco Polo? Do you think of a game you play in the swimming pool? Well, "Marco Polo" is a water game, but it is also the name of a very famous explorer who lived over seven hundred years ago!

Marco Polo started out in Italy and traveled all the way to the far Eastern coast of China. That is halfway around the world—and it is even more amazing that he did this with almost no roads or maps or guides. In fact, he actually walked a lot of the way—there were no cars or bicycles back then! It took him three years to get to China. He stayed for 24 years and it took him three more years to get back to Italy.

Marco Polo is famous for telling people in Europe about many amazing Chinese inventions and discoveries. For example, the Chinese people were already using paper money, while Europeans used only coins. The Chinese invented block printing for books, long before the Europeans figured it out. They knew how to burn coal, to make beautiful dishes (ever wonder why your mom calls it "china"?), and to weave silk from the cocoon of the silkworm caterpillar. They had even invented gunpowder, but they didn't use it for war. Instead, they used it to power their other famous invention—fireworks!

So the next time you are in the pool and someone yells "Marco," try to remember the wonderful things that Marco Polo taught the world about his friends in China. And *then* yell "Polo"!

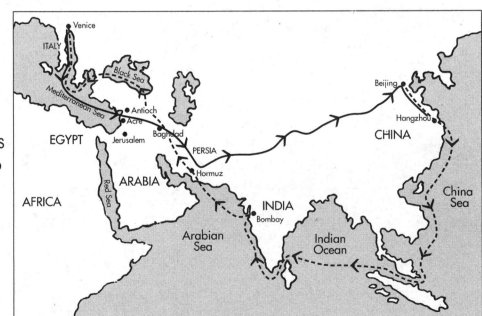

By Mary Rose

We completed this
assignment together.

_____

(Child's Signature)

_____

(Parent's Signature)

The Questions

✳ • ✳

Use two different colored pencils and the map on page 58. Have your parents help you use one color to trace the way Marco Polo went out to China and a different color to trace the path he used to get back to Italy.

Write down five new things the Chinese people showed to Marco Polo:

1. _____

2. _____

3. _____

4. _____

5. _____

Just for Fun

Passage	Skill	Standard
The History of Gum	Sequencing events in nonfiction	Arranges events in chronological order
Flag Facts	Gathering information; constructing meaning	Constructs meaning from reading selections
Puzzled by Puzzles?	Recognizing compare and contrast	Recognizes compare and contrast
Wham-O-Toys	Determining the main idea	Determines the main idea

he articles in this chapter are grouped into a category called "Just for Fun," because they contain information that most young children will find especially interesting. As was discussed in the Introduction, there are several ways to present the assignments in this book. If you are using them in chronological order, you will be introducing the stories in this chapter well into the school year. And that will work just fine.

Alternately, if you are picking and choosing articles and stories, you might wind up using this chapter in a piecemeal fashion. And that would work just fine, too. In this scenario, you might try pairing these homework assignments with activities in your classroom. Send home "Flag Facts" around Veterans Day or near Flag Day; present "Puzzled by Puzzles?" just before the winter holidays when students will have free time around the house to do jigsaw puzzles. Save "The History of Gum" and "Wham-O Toys" until just before spring or summer break so children can relate to vacation staples—Frisbees and bubble gum. No matter which way you approach this chapter, have fun!

The History of Gum

Skill Focus: Sequencing Events in Nonfiction

Traditionally, reading instruction in second and third grades focused almost exclusively on fiction. As students moved to fourth grade, they were abruptly confronted with a barrage of nonfiction from which they were supposed to be able to extract information in order to answer test questions. This, of course, proved to be difficult for students who had very little formal training in reading nonfiction. The "History of Gum" and other nonfiction pieces in this book have been included to help lay a firm foundation for younger students in reading and understanding informational texts.

Listing events in chronological order is often an overlooked skill with respect to nonfiction pieces. This article and the accompanying activities are intended to give your students practice in going back to an essay to find specific information. Students learn to make a connection between chronological numbering of years and the sequence of events in a piece of writing. At the same time, they practice the skill of searching out specific details in a piece of nonfiction.

If your school will allow, you can make this homework activity even more fun by bringing in samples of Dentyne, Chiclets, and Double Bubble gum.

Flag Facts

Skill Focus: Gathering Information; Constructing Meaning

One of the most difficult skills that students need to learn is that of gathering information from more than one source and then combining that information to answer a question. The activity about the American flag is intended to start students on their way to acquiring this skill. Students are asked to read the text and to draw and color a picture according to what they have understood.

Make this lesson even more meaningful by having a real flag for the students to look at before they take home the homework assignment. When the homework papers have been returned, see if you can involve your students in taking care of your school's flag for a week.

Puzzled by Puzzles?

Skill Focus: Recognizing Compare and Contrast

This story will give your students an opportunity to recognize the author's use of compare and contrast. They may be familiar with this skill when it comes to fiction pieces, but they may not have had much experience in recognizing the ways authors compare and contrast in nonfiction material. This activity also asks children to go back to the story to locate specific pieces of

Related Lessons

See additional lessons on Recognizing Compare and Contrast in "The Fire on the Mountain" on page 18, "The Little Red Hen" on page 26, and "Spaghetti Poems" on page 90.

information in order to answer a question. This is a valuable skill for insuring success on standardized tests

Make this lesson more interesting by borrowing a few puzzles from the kindergarten classroom. These puzzles will have four or five large pieces that fit into a shaped "puzzle tray." Show these to your class along with puzzles containing 30 to 100 or even 1000 pieces. If you can devote a corner of your classroom to a long-range project, set up a puzzle table for your students. Working on a puzzle can be a motivating quiet activity for students to choose when their regular assignments are completed. Using hands-on materials not only clarifies the information in nonfiction text, it makes reading more meaningful and fun for students. You can get more information about the history of jigsaw puzzles by going to www.mgcpuzzles.com.

Wham-O Toys

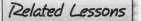

Skill Focus: Determining the Main Idea

No matter how much you practice this skill with your students, it is still difficult for many of them to clearly identify the main idea of a nonfiction story or article. Try to remember to have them state the main idea as a complete sentence. If students disagree about what the main idea of an article is, make sure you clarify it for them, and show them how you determined it. Do not leave the question open, or students will not develop a good feel for how to identify the main idea. It is also helpful to use the students' own words as you help the class sum up the main idea. When you use their words, you give validity to their ideas and let them know they are on the right track.

The original name for the Wham-O Toy company came from the sound made by their first toy—a sling shot. There are many other toys made by the Wham-O Toy company. Some of your students may have a Hacky Sack, a Boogie Board, or Silly String.

> **Related Lessons**
>
> See additional lessons on Determining the Main Idea in "The Three Billy Goats Gruff" on page 16, and "Danger Ahead: The American Alligator" on page 43.

The History of Gum

LISTEN to your child read this story aloud.

The history of gum began thousands of years ago when prehistoric men and women chewed lumps of tree resin (a sticky brown material that oozes from trees). The ancient Greeks chewed on resin, and so did Native Americans. Early settlers to New England loved to chew resin, too. In 1869, a man from New York named Thomas Adams invented gum as we know it today. He used *chicle*, which is the sap from a sapodilla tree. Soon everyone in New York was chewing!

Then a new product called Dentyne® came out. This chewing gum was supposed to be healthy for your teeth. Around 1900, someone covered pieces of Dentyne® gum with sugar and called the new product Chiclets.®

The first bubble gum, called Blibber-Blubber, was invented in 1906. It was so sticky that if a bubble popped on your face, it would not come off, so the company had to stop making it.

Finally, in 1928, Walter Diemer come up with the perfect bubble gum recipe. He invented Double Bubble,® the first real bubble gum. He made it pink because that was the only color of dye he had. He took a five-pound lump of the gum to a grocery store. It sold out that afternoon.

You can still buy Dentyne,® Chiclets,® and Double Bubble® bubble gum today—proof that some great things have been great for a very long time!

Abridged by Mary Rose from an article by Lauren Tarshis

Dear Parents,

Students are used to being asked to list events in chronological order when reading fictional stories. They are familiar with questions that ask them "What happened first, next, and last in the story?" But students also need to develop this same skill within the context of nonfiction pieces. As they advance through school, they will need to understand chronological order in content areas such as social studies and science. Because this is probably a new skill for your child, this assignment may prove somewhat difficult. After listening carefully as he or she reads aloud the passage about the history of gum, work together to find and list the historical events in the correct order.

We completed this
assignment together.

_____
(Child's Signature)

_____
(Parent's Signature)

The Questions

❋ • • • • • • • • • • • • • • • • • • • ❋

1. List four groups of people who chewed gum before it was invented in 1869.

_____   _____

_____   _____

2. List three brands of gum in the order in which they were created.
(**Hint:** Remember that a brand name begins with a capital letter.)

_____   _____

_____

3. In what year did Thomas Adams create chicle gum? _____

4. In what year did Walter Diemer create Double Bubble® bubble gum? _____

5. Which was invented first, chicle gum or bubble gum? _____

Flag Facts

LISTEN to your child read this story aloud.

Do you know why your school puts up the flag every day? In 1800, James B. Upham wanted schoolchildren to save pennies to buy American flags for their schools. Today the flag is always flown when children are in class.

Do you know why the flag is only halfway up the flagpole sometimes? When the flag is only halfway up, it is called flying at "half-staff." (The staff is the flagpole.) This is done to honor someone important who has died.

Do you know that sometimes the flag was flown upside down on a flagpole? When the flag was put up this way on a ship at sea, it was a way to tell others that the ship needed help.

Do you know we have a special day to honor our flag? It is June 14 every year.

Do you know why our flag is red, white, and blue? The red stands for bravery, the white stands for innocence and purity, and the blue stands for justice. These are among the most important qualities valued by our country.

Do you know any rules about handling the flag? The American flag should never touch the ground. It should always be flown higher than other flags. You should put the flag up quickly and take it down slowly. If the flag is not made of plastic, it should not get wet. The flag should not be flown at night unless there is a light shining on it.

By Mary Rose

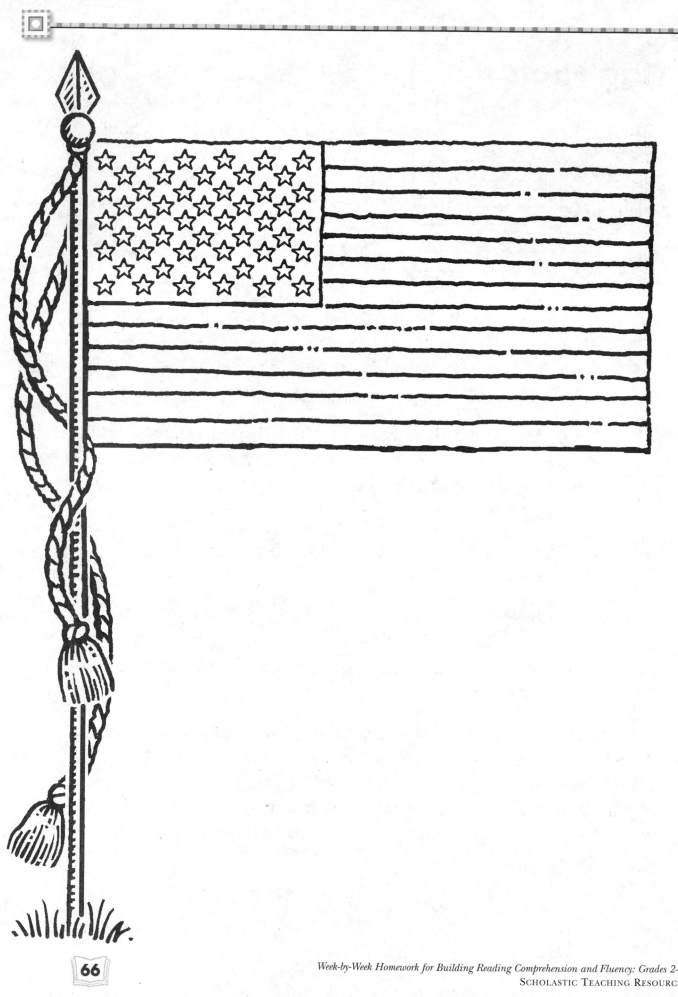

Dear Parents,

This assignment calls on your child to gather information from material that is written in a question-and-answer format. The child is asked to find certain facts from that material and write answers for each question using those facts. This is a good opportunity to teach your child an important lesson: readers, both young and older, are not expected to remember everything they read. The trick is to focus on what is important while one is reading and to know how to skim and scan the material afterward to gather the key information.

Have your child go back to the article and underline the answer to each question. Then help him or her write an answer using his or her own words.

We completed this
assignment together.

_____

(Child's Signature)

_____

(Parent's Signature)

The Questions

Color the flag on page 66. The top and bottom stripes should both be red. The space between the stars should be blue.

1. What do these colors stand for? _____

_____

2. What is the rule for flying the flag at night? _____

_____

3. What is the rule for putting the flag up correctly? _____

_____

4. What is the day we honor the flag each year? _____

_____

5. What does it mean if the flag is flying at half-staff? _____

_____

Puzzled by Puzzles?

LISTEN to your child read this story aloud.

When you were very young, you probably put together wooden jigsaw puzzles that had pieces about as large as your hand. Each puzzle had about four or five pieces, and each piece fit into a space all by itself. The pieces might not even touch each other in the finished puzzle. By now you have probably learned to like jigsaw puzzles that have many small pieces. And in a few years, you may be doing really hard puzzles—ones with a thousand pieces!

The first jigsaw puzzles were made in 1760—even before America was a country. People in Europe pasted maps onto wood and then cut them apart. The trick was to put the map back together to make a country.

In the early 1900s, people really started to love wooden jigsaw puzzles, but they were not very much like our modern cardboard ones. For one thing, the pieces did not lock together. One little bump, and the whole puzzle would fall apart. Often there was no picture on the lid or the puzzle box. This made it really hard to put the puzzle together. The finished picture was always a surprise.

In the 1930s, The Parker Brothers Company made their puzzles more fun by cutting the pieces into shapes like children, dogs, numbers, and flowers. During the Great Depression people bought ten million puzzles a week. If they didn't have enough money to buy one, they could rent one at the library for three cents. Puzzles sometimes came free when you bought something else, much like the prizes in cereal boxes today.

Today the most famous puzzles are made by The Stave Puzzle Company. They cut all of their puzzles by hand and will even cut a piece shaped like your name. They make trick puzzles that will go together more than one way. Some of the Stave puzzles cost as much as $4,000!

Puzzles have come a long way since the first ones were invented. You, too, have come a long way since you first fit that giant puzzle piece into its special place.

By Mary Rose

Dear Parents,

This article about jigsaw puzzles uses the literary convention of compare and contrast, even though the clues to this are fairly subtle. Nowhere does the article state that one thing is being directly compared to another. If you (and your child) look carefully, however, you'll notice that throughout the article the author compares how puzzles used to be with the way they are now. Remember (as with earlier assignments of this nature, "The Fire on the Mountain" and "The Little Red Hen") your child is not being asked to actually do the comparing, but instead is expected to recognize when an author has used this convention. Once again, it may be easier for your child if he or she highlights or underlines the information in the passage.

Skill

Recognizing Compare and Contrast

We completed this assignment together.

_____
(Child's Signature)

_____
(Parent's Signature)

The Questions

The author compares older jigsaw puzzles to new ones. See if you can find four ways the author tells you that puzzles are the same and different.

1. What are jigsaw puzzles made of?

Old ones: _____ New ones: _____

2. How do the puzzle boxes look?

Old ones: _____ New ones: _____

3. How does the puzzle stay together?

Old ones: _____ New ones: _____

4. How much does the puzzle cost?

Old ones: _____ New ones: _____

Bonus: Did you find more things that are the same or more that are different?

Wham-O® Toys

LISTEN to your child read this story aloud.

Do the names Richard Knerr and Arthur "Spud" Melin mean anything to you? You have probably never heard of them, but in 1948, these two men started the Wham-O® toy company, and the company is still making toys today.

In the 1950s, these men heard about people using circles made from bamboo to help with exercise and losing weight. The men thought kids would like to play with the circles too. They made their circles out of hollow plastic. They made 25 million of their toys in the first two months. After a few years they had sold 100 million. What do you think the toy was?

Another toy made by the Wham-O® toy company really started out as a pie pan. It became popular for young people to toss around the pie pans from the Frisbie Pie Company, after they had eaten the pie. This gave Fred Morrison an idea. He made a toy shaped like these pans, using plastic instead of metal. He called it the "Pluto Platter," but people didn't buy very many of them. Then he changed the name of the toy. In 1957, he began selling his new toy. You can still buy this toy today. Can you guess what it is?

A third toy from Wham-O® is much newer. Children often play with this toy in the summer, and when they do, they get really wet. No, it is not a garden hose. It is not a plastic pool. It is not a water gun. Here's a hint: You lie on your tummy and slide on it. Now do you know what toy it is?

This summer you can thank the Wham-O® toy company for making your life more fun!

By Mary Rose

Dear Parents,

Students need to be able to determine the main idea, or essential message, in both fiction and nonfiction. The name of this company is probably completely unfamiliar to your child. But as he or she figures out the identity of famous Wham-O® toys (with your help and with the help of the illustrations), one thing should become quite clear: The Wham-O® toy company has been making popular and fun toys for a long time. And, simple as it may seem, this is the "essential message" of the article—that this toy company constantly works to create new, fun toys for children to play with.

We completed this assignment together.

_____
(Child's Signature)

_____
(Parent's Signature)

The Questions

❋ • ❋

1. What are three toys made by the Wham-O® toy company?

_____   _____

_____

2. What is the main thing you will remember about the Wham-O® toy company?

_____

_____

3. What is your favorite Wham-O® toy? (**Hint:** Look around at home to see if you have any that are not in this story!)

_____

Poetry and Figurative Language

Passage	Skill	Standard
"Let's Marry!" said the Cherry	Identifying rhyming words and couplets	Recognizes effects of language such as rhyme
Old Mother Hubbard	Identifying rhyming words; factual recall	Recognizes effects of language such as rhyme; factual recall
Rain Sizes	Understanding figurative language: similes	Understands/interprets figurative language; uses literary terms
Three Blind Mice	Using context clues	Uses context clues
The Llama and the Aardvark	Retelling in prose; using context clues	Constructs meaning; uses context clues
December Leaves	Understanding figurative language: metaphors	Understands/interprets figurative language; uses literary terms
Spaghetti Poems	Comparing and contrasting in poetry	Compares works of literature to each other

any teachers may not be aware that on standardized tests poetry is treated the same as prose, and that all benchmarks and standards that apply to prose also apply to poetry. This chapter of homework assignments asks students to apply their literary skills to poetry. The pieces in this chapter should, we hope, appeal to teachers, parents, and especially to children.

Remember that each poem needs to be read out loud several times before students can get the flow of words or understand the subtle meanings hidden within. Have the children do some choral reading to practice pausing where there is punctuation—not necessarily at the end of the line. Be sure to use terms such as *stanza* and *rhyme*. Try having students paraphrase a poem in their own words. If they can do this successfully, then you can assume that they understand it.

Be sure to present lots of poetry to your students in the course of your own regular classroom instruction. Young children should experience this particularly creative and inventive genre, have fun with it, and begin to revel in word play and word fun as early as possible.

"Let's Marry!" said the Cherry

Skill Focus: Identifying Rhyming Words and Couplets

Make sure to do some rhyming activities before you send this page home. Young children really enjoy the sounds and flow of rhyming word patterns. Try teaching them some jump rope songs to help them feel the way the words in a rhyming poem go together.

After you have completed this homework page, try talking to your students in rhyming couplets, such as "'Go to lunch,' said the bunch" or "'Time to read,' said the bead." Let your students respond to you in the same patterns. This word play is not just for fun. It helps your students to understand how words work and to appreciate the variety in our language.

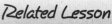

Related Lesson

See additional lesson on Identifying Rhyming Words in "Old Mother Hubbard" on page 79.

Old Mother Hubbard

Skill Focus: Identifying Rhyming Words; Factual Recall

Children will enjoy hearing the longer version of this familiar poem. Make sure they understand the last verse.

If time allows, ask students to illustrate a favorite verse, or assign different students to write a verse at the top of the page and illustrate it. Staple these together to create a class book. To get students started, ask questions like: *Where would Old Mother Hubbard have gone today? What would she be getting for her dog?* If they need further help, provide poetry line stems like these:

Related Lesson

See additional lesson on Identifying Rhyming Words in "Let's Marry! said the Cherry" on page 76.

○ She went to the supermarket to get him a . . .

○ She went to a restaurant to get him . . .

○ She went to a toy store to get him a . . .

○ She went to the backyard to get him . . .

Related Lesson

See additional lesson on Factual Recall in "Marco Polo" on page 58.

Rain Sizes

Skill Focus: Understanding Figurative Language: Similes

Similes (comparisons that use *like* or *as*) are an important part of our language. There are a number of clever similes for rain in John Ciardi's poem ("Some rain is as big as a nickel" or "And tingles as if you'd been kissed.") They are simple and tactile enough for even young children to understand. Authors frequently use similes when describing actions or when giving physical descriptions of places or characters. This lesson is designed to call attention to similes and to present some familiar ones to students. Create a chart that lists similes you find during whole-class read alouds and allow students to add similes they encounter in their independent reading. Encourage students to use similes in their conversations and in their written work.

Three Blind Mice

Skill Focus: Using Context Clues

We typically expect students to read passages and discern meaning from context clues. But if we expect them to do this with selections that are written at a difficult reading level, they will most often guess incorrectly at the meanings of unfamiliar words. By using a familiar, singsong poem that most young children (and their parents) know, students will have an opportunity to practice getting information from context clues in a fun and nonthreatening way.

You may want to begin this lesson by reading aloud the seventh stanza of this poem. This is the one that is most familiar to students.

Related Lesson

See additional lesson on Using Context Clues in "The Llama and the Aardvark" on page 86.

The Llama and the Aardvark

Skill Focus: Retelling in Prose; Using Context Clues

This simple poem offers opportunities to practice several skills. Students can learn to recognize the correct spelling of *llama* and *aardvark*; they can have fun experiencing the meaning of "poetic license"; they can practice using context clues for unfamiliar words; and they can practice retelling the poem in prose. You may want to preface this assignment with lessons about other "word play" poetry. The poems of Jack Prelutsky and Shel Silverstein are particularly appealing to children and offer the same kinds of opportunities for fun with words.

Related Lesson

See additional lesson on Using Context Clues in "Three Blind Mice" on page 83.

December Leaves

Skill Focus: Understanding Figurative Language: Metaphors

Along with the earlier lesson on similes, this assignment is intended as a "starter" page for understanding figurative language. The poem, "December Leaves," is a wonderful introduction to a particular kind of figurative language, metaphors. In a simple manner, it presents five clever metaphors that even young children should be able to understand. (Fallen leaves are cornflakes; the lawn is a wide dish; the wind is a stirring spoon; the sky is a silver sifter; and the snow is sugar.) However, because the concept of metaphors is more difficult than similes for most children to grasp (it does not employ a comparative word, but simply states that something *is* something else), you may decide not to use the term itself. Instead, you might just let your students realize that the poet has compared a number of things in nature to other things and let them enjoy the variety of images created.

Spaghetti Poems

Skill Focus: Comparing and Contrasting in Poetry

This lesson focuses on the skill of comparing and contrasting. However, there are two key differences between this lesson and previous lessons on this same skill. First, here we are asking the children themselves to do the comparing and contrasting, not to simply recognize an author's comparisons. Second, the fact that the skill now applies to poetry, rather than prose, gives it a different slant.

Children usually enjoy the rhythm of poems like these, and they should have some additional fun comparing the two poems' descriptions of spaghetti. Help students to realize that just about all basic reading skills, including the ability to compare and contrast, are relevant to all forms of literature.

> **Related Lessons**
>
> See additional lessons on Comparing and Contrasting in "The Fire on the Mountain" on page 18, "The Little Red Hen" on page 26, and "Puzzled by Puzzles?" on page 68.

"Let's Marry!" said the Cherry

LISTEN to your child read this poem aloud.

"Let's marry!"
said the cherry.

"Why me?"
said the pea.

"'Cause you're sweet,"
said the beet.

"Say you will,"
said the dill.

"Think it over,"
said the clover.

"Don't rush,"
said the squash.

"Here's your dress,"
said the cress.

"White and green,"
said the bean.

"And your cape,"
said the grape.

"Trimmed with fur,"
said the burr.

"Won't that tickle?"
said the pickle.

"Who knows?"
said the rose.

"Where's the chapel?"
said the apple.

"In Greenwich,"
said the spinach.

"We'll be there!"
said the pear.

"Wearing what?"
said the nut.

"Pants and coats,"
said the oats.

"Shoes and socks,"
said the phlox.

By N.M. Bodecker

Week-by-Week Homework for Building Reading Comprehension and Fluency: Grades 2–3
SCHOLASTIC TEACHING RESOURCES

"I'll chime!"
said the thyme.

"Who will preach?"
said the peach.

"It's my turn!"
said the fern.

"You would ramble,"
said the bramble.

"Shirt and tie,"
said the rye.

"Here they come!"
said the plum.

"We'll look jolly,"
said the holly.

"Start the tune!"
cried the prune.

"You'll look silly,"
said the lily.

"All together!"
cried the heather.

"You're crazy,"
said the daisy.

"Here we go!"
said the sloe.

"Come, let's dine,"
said the vine.

"Now—let's marry!"
said the cherry.

"Yeah—let's eat!"
said the wheat.

"Why me?"
said the pea.

"And get stout,"
said the sprout.

"Oh, my gosh!"
said the squash.

"Just wait,"
said the date.

"Start all over,"
said the clover.

"Who will chime?"
said the lime.

"NO WAY!"
said the hay.

Dear Parents,

It would be wise for you to read this particular poem out loud to your child the first time through. It will help him or her understand the events of the story. Then try reading it again, taking turns. One of you can read the part in quotation marks, and the other can read the speaker tags. For example, you read, "Let's marry!" and your child reads, "said the cherry." Taking turns like this allows your child to hear the rhyming word clearly. It's also an aid as he or she tries to make an educated guess at unfamiliar words (of which there will be quite a few in this poem). If your child says a word that is not in the story, guide him or her to look at the beginning and ending sounds to try to get the word right. Finally, ask your child to read the whole poem out loud on his or her own.

We completed this
assignment together.

_____
(Child's Signature)

_____
(Parent's Signature)

The Questions

Did you know that the word *couple* means "two"? This poem is made up of rhyming couplets. That means that the two lines go together and the last word in each line rhymes. Make a list of the rhyming words from the poem on the spaces below.

marry _____   chapel _____

me _____   crazy _____

_____ oats   _____ peach

_____ burr   wait _____

jolly _____   turn _____

Now write two rhyming couplets of your own. They can be silly!

_____

_____

_____

Old Mother Hubbard

LISTEN to your child read this poem aloud.

Old Mother Hubbard
Went to the cupboard
To get her poor dog a bone.
But when she came there
The cupboard was bare,
And so the poor dog had none.

She took a clean dish
To get him some tripe,
But when she came back
He was smoking his pipe.

She went to the fishmonger's
To buy him some fish,
And when she came back
He was licking the dish.

She went to the hatter's
To buy him a hat,
But when she came back
He was feeding her cat.

She went to the barber's
To buy him a wig,
But when she came back
He was dancing a jig.

She went to the fruiterer's
To buy him some fruit,
But when she came back
He was playing the flute.

She went to the tailor's
To buy him a coat,
But when she came back
He was riding a goat.

She went to the cobbler's
To buy him some shoes,
But when she came back
He was reading the news.

She went to the hosier's
To buy him some hose,
But when she came back
He was dressed in his clothes.

The dame made a curtsey,
The dog made a bow;
The dame said, "Your servant,"
The dog said," Bow, wow."

A Mother Goose rhyme

Dear Parents,

This timeless rhyme speaks to everyone, but perhaps best to the pet owners among us, who can surely relate to this story of an old lady and her dog. How many doting owners have "bent over backwards" to make a pet happy? Discuss with your child who is in charge here by examining the final verse and the meanings of unfamiliar words like dame and curtsey. Read this poem several times with your child. Try omitting the final word in each stanza, encouraging your child to guess at it by supplying a rhyming word.

In addition to focusing on rhyming words, this lesson highlights another, quite different skill— recalling specific facts. This key ability needs to be developed in all genres of literature, including poetry.

We completed this
assignment together.

_____

(Child's Signature)

_____

(Parent's Signature)

The Questions

* • *

1. Name three things that Old Mother Hubbard did for her dog.

_____

_____

_____

2. Name three things the dog did.

_____

_____

_____

3. What do you think is the meaning of the word *dame*? _____

4. What is the meaning of the word *curtsey*? _____

Rain Sizes

LISTEN to your child read this poem aloud.

Rain comes in various sizes.
Some rain is as small as a mist.
It tickles your face with surprises,
And tingles as if you'd been kissed.

Some rain is the size of a sprinkle
And doesn't put out all the sun.
You can see the drops sparkle and twinkle,
And a rainbow comes out when it's done.

Some rain is as big as a nickel
And comes with a crash and a hiss.
It comes down too heavy to tickle.
It's more like a splash than a kiss.

When it rains the right size and you're wrapped in
Your rainclothes, it's fun out of doors.
But run home before you get trapped in
The big rain that rattles and roars.

By John Ciardi

Dear Parents,

Each of the phrases listed in the Questions section below is a simile. A simile is a comparison that uses like or as. The first set of similes is taken from the poem in this lesson, "Rain Sizes." Help your child to enjoy the poet's clever comparisons and other unusual word usage. Even the concept of rain having a size is fun and different! Then help your child to complete the matching activity. The similes listed should be familiar to you, and hopefully, to your child, too. Read each phrase out loud as you complete it. More importantly, please use lots of similes when you are talking with your child. It's also important to point them out when you are reading stories. If you start to look for them, you'll find similes in places you never noticed before!

We completed this
assignment together.

_____
(Child's Signature)

_____
(Parent's Signature)

The Questions

❊ • ❊

1. Read the poem a second time. Find the three lines listed below and fill in the similes that the poet uses.

   And tingles as if _____.

   Some rain is as big as a _____.

   It's more like a _____ than a kiss.

2. Here are some new similes. Fill in the blank space of each simile with a word from the column on the right. Be sure to spell correctly!

It's as sour as a _____.	lightning
That puppy is as cute as a _____.	ice
He's as fast as _____.	firecracker
This candy is as hard as a _____.	molasses
He runs as slow as _____.	grass
Her shirt is as green as _____.	lemon
The sidewalk is as hot as a _____.	button
The soup is as cold as _____.	rock

Three Blind Mice

LISTEN to your child read this poem aloud.

Three Small Mice
Pined for some fun.
They made up their mind to set out to roam.
Said they, "It's dull to remain at home."
And all they took with them was a comb,
Three Small Mice.

Three Starved Mice
Came to a farm,
The farmer was eating some bread and cheese,
So they all went down on their hands and knees,
And squeaked, "Pray, give us a morsel, please,"
These Three Starved Mice.

Three Glad Mice
Ate all they could.
They felt so happy they danced with glee,
But the farmer's wife came in to see
What might this merry-making be
Of Three Glad Mice.

Three Poor Mice,
Soon changed their tune,
The farmer's wife said, "What are you at
And why were you capering around like that?
Just wait a minute, I'll fetch the cat,"
Oh dear, Poor Mice.

Three Scared Mice
Ran for their lives.
They jumped out on to the window ledge,
The mention of "Cat" set their teeth on edge,
So they hid themselves in the bramble hedge,
These Three Scared Mice.

Three Sad Mice,
What could they do?
The bramble hedge was most unkind
It scratched their eyes and made them blind,
And soon each Mouse went out of his mind,
These Three Sad Mice.

Three Blind Mice,
See how they run.
They all run after the farmer's wife.
She cut off their tails with a carving knife.
Did you ever see such a sight in your life?
As Three Blind Mice?

Three Sick Mice,
Gave way to tears,
They could not see and they had no end,
They sought a chemist and found a friend,
He gave them some "Never Too Late to Mend,"
These Three Sick Mice.

Three Wise Mice
Rubbed, rubbed away.
And soon their tails began to grow,
And their eyes recovered their sight, you know
They looked in the glass and it told them so
These Three Wise Mice.

Three Proud Mice,
Soon settled down.
The name of their house, I cannot tell.
But they've learned a trade and are doing well,
If you call on them, please ring the bell
Three times twice.

By John W. Ivimey
(Excerpted from Complete Version of *Ye Three Blind Mice*)

84

Dear Parents,

You might start this assignment by telling your child that he or she has probably never heard this complete poem. The seventh stanza is the only part of "The Three Blind Mice" that is really well known. (Even this version is not complete.)

As you and your child read the poem, try doing so in the sing-song way that is so familiar. Thus, you would repeat the first two lines of each stanza. For instance, for the first stanza, you would read, "Three Small Mice/Three Small Mice/ Pined for some fun./Pined for some fun./ They made up their mind to set out to roam..." (and so on). Try to remember to do this with the first two lines of every stanza.

We completed this assignment together.

_____

(Child's Signature)

_____

(Parent's Signature)

The Questions

❋ · ❋

Reread the verses that contain these words. Together, use context clues in the verse to help you guess the meanings of the words and phrases below. Write your best guess on the line.

roam _____

morsel_____

glee _____

capering _____

bramble hedge _____

carving _____

"gave way to tears" _____

"they had no end" _____

Bonus: What is "Never Too Late to Mend"? _____

What do you think they were doing when they "rubbed, rubbed away"?

_____

The Llama and the Aardvark

LISTEN to
your child read
this poem aloud.

The llama aand the aardvark
   Went aambling by the llake;
The llama said, "I llove you
   Aas much aas llemon cake."
The llady aardvark aanswered,
   "I've lloved you aall aalong,
"Aas much aas llarks and llovebirds
   "Aadore aan Aapril song."

The llama said, "How llovely!
   "Llet's never llive aapart."
The aalways-aardent aardvark
   Aagreed with aall her heart.

By Leslie D. Perkins

Week-by-Week Homework for Building Reading Comprehension and Fluency: Grades 2–3
SCHOLASTIC TEACHING RESOURCES

Dear Parents,

Because reading is based on recognizing familiar letter patterns, at first glance this poem may be difficult to read. In the English language, we do not, for instance, expect two a's at the beginning of a word. You may need to help your child recognize the word play that the poet has used. Then help him or her make informed guesses about the meanings of any unfamiliar words.

One way to know if children have understood poetry is to ask them to retell the poem using prose. If children can tell the story in their own words, it means that they understood the poem. The second part of the activity below asks your child to retell the story so that you can check for understanding.

We completed this assignment together.

_____

(Child's Signature)

_____

(Parent's Signature)

The Questions

1. This poem uses words that you might not know. What is the meaning of each of the following words? Write your best guess on the line.

   ambling _____

   adore _____

   ardent _____

2. What do you notice about the spelling of the words *llama* and *aardvark*?

   _____

3. The poet noticed this too. How can you tell?

   _____

4. Using your own words, retell the story that the poem tells.

   _____

   _____

LISTEN to
your child read
this poem aloud.

December Leaves

The fallen leaves are cornflakes
That fill the lawn's wide dish,
And night and noon
The wind's a spoon
That stirs them with a swish.
The sky's a silver sifter,
A-sifting white and slow,
That gently shakes
On crisp brown flakes
The sugar known as snow.

By Kaye Starbird

Skill

Understanding Figurative Language: Metaphors

We completed this assignment together.

_____

(Child's Signature)

_____

(Parent's Signature)

The Questions

In this poem, the poet says that something is something else. For instance, she says that the wind is a spoon. Find four more places where she does this in the poem. On the lines below, write what the poet has said.

1. The leaves are _____.

2. The lawn is a _____.

3. The sky is a _____.

4. The snow is _____.

Now try to write your own comparisons. Get Mom or Dad to help. What do the following things suggest to you?

5. Bare trees are _____.

6. Brown grass is _____.

7. Gray sky is _____.

8. Hanging icicles are _____.

9. Drifted snow is _____.

Spaghetti Poems

LISTEN to your child read this poem aloud.

Spaghetti! Spaghetti!

Spaghetti! Spaghetti!
You're wonderful stuff,
I love you, spaghetti,
I can't get enough.
You're covered with sauce
and you're sprinkled with cheese,
Spaghetti! Spaghetti!
Oh, give me some more please.

Spaghetti! Spaghetti!
Piled high in a mound,
you wiggle, you wriggle,
you squiggle around.
There's slurpy spaghetti
all over my plate,
Spaghetti! Spaghetti!
I think you are great.

Spaghetti! Spaghetti!
I love you a lot,
you're slishy, you're sloshy,
delicious and hot.
I gobble you down,
oh, I can't get enough.
Spaghetti! Spaghetti!
You're wonderful stuff.

By Jack Prelutsky

The Spaghetti Challenge

My mom's spaghetti is the best;
no other mom can beat it;
and every time she cooks it
I can hardly wait to eat it.

I twist the strands around my fork
with wonderful control,
but as I raise them to my mouth
they fall back in the bowl.

I twirl the noodles once again
with all the skill I'm able,
but as I lift them up to eat
they tumble to the table.

I spin my fork; spaghetti winds
around and round once more;
but as it nears my waiting lips
it slithers to the floor.

My mom's spaghetti is the best;
no other mom can beat it;
but I would like it better
if I got a chance to eat it.

By Leslie D. Perkins

Dear Parents,

Kids love spaghetti. Even the word—spaghetti—is fun to say! These two poems have been selected to give your child an opportunity to complete a compare and contrast activity within the context of poetry. (This skill is also important in fiction and nonfiction genres as you may recall from several previous homework assignments.) Please help your child recognize the similarities in the two poems, both those that are real and implied.

Also, you should be aware that this is the only assignment in which your child is asked to make the comparisons himself or herself. In the previous lessons, we asked children to identify comparisons made by the author. Both skills are important for your child to become a competent reader.

We completed this assignment together.

_____

(Child's Signature)

_____

(Parent's Signature)

The Questions

✳ • • • • • • • • • • • • • • • • • • ✳

Together, answer these questions about both spaghetti poems.

1. How does the speaker in each poem feel about spaghetti?

Poem # 1: _____

Poem # 2: _____

2. What words tell you how they feel about it?

Poem # 1: _____

Poem # 2: _____

3. What problem does the person in the second poem have? _____

_____

4. How are the two poems different? _____

_____

Answers

Answers to Questions on Page 17:

Answers will vary. Check that students have written details that were given in the story. Possible statements include: There was a Little (or Middle-Sized or Biggest) Billy Goat. They crossed a bridge. The Billy Goats talked the troll into waiting for the Biggest Billy Goat. The Biggest Billy Goat knocked the troll into the water.

Answers to Questions on Page 19:

1. Haptom is rich and is the master; Arha is poor and is the servant. 2. At the end of the story, they are both rich and (implied) Arha is no longer a servant. 3. Arha is on a mountaintop in the cold and freezing weather. 4. Haptom is at a party where dinner is being served. 5. The night that Arha is being tested, he passes the test because he can see the light of a fire. 6. The night Haptom is being tested, he realizes that smelling food does not make one full, just as seeing the fire didn't make Arha warm.

Answers to Questions on Page 21:

Answers will vary. Possible answers include:
1. The ant worked and saved food all summer.
2. The grasshopper played and sang all summer.
3. When winter came, the ant had food and the grasshopper did not. 4. You should work and save up for the bad times.
(*Additional Note:* In the course of discussion, many children will likely say that the ant should have shared with the grasshopper. You may want to point out that if the ant had done that, they would probably have both died because there wouldn't have been enough food for either of them.)

Answers to Questions on Page 23:

Answers may vary; accept all that are reasonable. Suggestions for circled sentences: Red—Once upon a time there was a prince who was looking for a real princess to marry. Blue—The queen put one single pea on the girl's bed. Green—The prince married the princess and they lived happily ever after.

Illustration should clearly show a girl, a bed, a pea, and twenty mattresses. The princess can be beside the bed, or on the bed.

Answers to Questions on Page 25:

1. The cause of the man's problem was too many coconuts. Or, the more he hurried his horse, the more the coconuts fell off. 2. The effect of moving the horse faster was that the coconuts kept falling off. 3. He tried to solve the problem by going faster and faster to make up for the lost time. 4. The sentence was true because if the man had walked the horse slowly, the coconuts would not have fallen and he would have arrived home sooner. He wasted a lot of time picking up the coconuts over and over again, so by hurrying, it took him longer.

Answers to Questions on Page 27:

Answers will vary. Possible answers include: 1. The little red hen is different from her friends because she is hardworking. Her friends are lazy and want something for nothing. The little red hen is willing to work for what she wants—bread. 2. The little red hen is like her friends because they all live in the same place and they all like bread. 3. The lesson is that you must work for the things you like. You should not expect others to do work for you. You should cooperate with others so you can share in the riches of hard work.

Answers to Questions on Page 29:

Answers will vary. Possible answers include:
1. The main problem is that the camel refuses to do any work for people, and the other animals think this is unfair. 2. The Djinn helped the animals solve their problem by giving the camel a hump and making him work in the desert. 3. Camel learned that everyone has to contribute and share the work.

Answers to Questions on Page 31:

Answers will vary. Possible answers include:
1. The dog was blown away from her family in a tornado. 2. She wandered around until a lady found her and took her home. 3. The lady gave

the dog to Lana, who named her Snuggles.

Answers to Questions on Page 33:

1. Michael's parents expected him to drive his real race car around the track. 2. Answers will vary. 3. He made a racetrack for his little toy cars. Then he sat down to play with the cars. He did not race his bigger car. 4. Michael told his mother, "I need to drive my cars." (The use of plural is the key here; Michael was referring to his little race cars all along.) 5. Michael's parents thought it was funny. I know because they were laughing.

Answers to Questions on Page 38:

kindly: kind, ly; useful: use, ful; tossed: toss, ed; finally: final, ly; named: name, ed; strutting: strut, (t)ing. Additional words the student might find include: called, homing, used, especially, released, actually, waiting, missing, legged, treated, honored, lived, received

Answers to Questions on Page 40:

1. It is a beautiful bird. 2. The eagle is amazing. 3. That good vision means that the eagle is wonderful. 4. The eagle would probably be a very unhappy bird if it didn't have those claws. 5. It could probably eat any fish it wanted in five minutes by using that beak. 6. The bald eagle is the best bird in the country.

Answers to Questions on Page 42:

1. This article is mainly about snow and snow crystals. 2. Answers will vary. Accept any answers that illustrate student has absorbed information from the article. 3. The theme of this article is that snow is fascinating and has many unusual qualities.

Answers to Questions on Page 44:

1. "Danger Ahead: The American Alligator" 2. The main idea of the article is that American alligators are very dangerous. 3. Answers will vary. Possible answers include: the alligator will attack humans; it moves fast; it has strong jaws and sharp teeth; it can drown its prey; it is especially aggressive in the spring.

Answers to Questions on Page 46:

1. B 2. Answers will vary, but may include the following: The author tells that the sloth lives most of its life upside down; that it cannot walk; that algae live in its fur and make it green; that its fur grows opposite of the way a dog's fur grows; that it eats, sleeps, and has babies upside down. Sloth should be colored green.

Answers to Questions on Page 51:

1. patriots: people who did not like the king of England; Charlestown: a town across the Charles River from Boston; Concord: a town 18 miles away; regulars: the king's soldiers from England; redcoats: British soldiers dressed in bright red uniforms. 2. Answers will vary.

Answers to Questions on Page 53:

Answers will vary. Possible answers include: 1. Butch O'Hare was brave when he attacked a group of Japanese fighter planes all by himself. He was brave when he did not give up. He kept fighting even after he had run out of bullets. He kept flying even after his plane was damaged. 2. Butch O'Hare acted so bravely because he cared so much for the lives of his fellow soldiers. 3. Possible answers: The effect of Butch O'Hare's bravery was that the lives of several thousand men were saved. The aircraft carrier was saved. He was decorated as a hero. An airport was named after him.

Answers to Questions on Page 55:

1. elevate: lift 2. started: began 3. unsafe: dangerous 4. tall: towering 5. built: erected 6. ride: convey

Answers to Questions on Page 57:

Past tense verbs: walked, noticed, shouted, offered, stepped, lifted, looked, asked, unbuttoned, showed, helped, realized. Present tense verbs: know, think, am, aren't, have, send (Note: If students write infinitives, such as "to make" and "to see" in second paragraph, you might explain that these are forms of verbs they haven't studied yet and that they should go back to the story to find verbs that do fit the lesson.)

Answers to Questions on Page 59:

Check map to see that child traced the paths correctly. 1–5. Answers will vary, but should include five of the following: paper money, fireworks, burning coal, china dishes, silk, gunpowder, and block printing.

Answers to Questions on Page 64:

1. prehistoric people, ancient Greeks, Native Americans, and early settlers to New England 2. Dentyne, Chiclets, and Blibber-Blubber bubble gum. 3. 1869 4. 1928 5. chicle gum

Answers to Questions on Page 67:

Check that the flag is appropriately colored. 1. Red stands for bravery, blue stands for justice, and white stands for purity or innocence. 2. A flag needs to be lit if it is to be flown at night. 3. The flag should be put up quickly. 4. June 14. 5. A flag is flown at half-staff to honor someone who has died.

Answers to Questions on Page 69:

1. Old ones: wood; New ones: wood or cardboard 2. Old ones: plain with no picture; New ones: picture 3. Old ones: did not stay together; New ones: have locking pieces 4. Old ones: rent for 3 cents or get for free; New ones: cost more money
Bonus: More things that are different

Answers to Questions on Page 71:

1. The Hula Hoop, the Frisbee, and the Slip 'n Slide 2. Answers will vary. Possible answer: The main thing I will remember is that the Wham-O toy company makes toys. Children may also mention that the company makes lots of toys or that it has been around for a long time. 3. Answers will vary.

Answers to Questions on Page 78:

marry: cherry; me: pea; coats: oats; fur: burr; jolly: holly; chapel: apple; crazy: daisy; preach: peach; wait: date; turn: fern
Children's couplets will vary. They are correct if the words at the end of each line rhyme.

Answers to Questions on Page 80:

1. Answers will vary. Possible answers include: She went to the cupboard to get him a bone; she took a clean dish to get him some tripe (stomach lining of an animal); she went to the fishmonger's to buy him some fish; she went to the hatter's to buy him a hat; she went to the barber's to buy him a wig; she went to the fruiterer's to buy him some fruit; she went to the tailor's to buy him a coat; she went to the cobbler's to buy him some shoes; and she went to the hosier's to buy him some hose. 2. Possible answers include: The dog smoked a pipe; licked a dish; fed the cat; danced a jig; played the flute; rode a goat; read the news; and dressed in his clothes. Then he said, "Bow, wow." 3. *Dame* means "woman." 4. *Curtsey* means "to bow."

Answers to Questions on Page 82:

1. you'd been kissed; nickel; splash 2. It's as sour as a lemon. That puppy is as cute as a button. He's as fast as lightning. This candy is as hard as a rock. He runs as slow as molasses. Her shirt is as green as grass. The sidewalk is as hot as a firecracker. The soup is as cold as ice.

Answers to Questions on Page 85:

Answers will vary. Possible answers include: roam: wander about; morsel: small bite of food; glee: happiness, giddiness; capering: dancing; bramble hedge: sticker bush; carving: cutting up meat; "gave way to tears": began crying "they had no end": their tails were gone
Bonus: "Never Too Late to Mend" was the medicine that fixed their eyes and made their tails grow back.

Answers to Questions on Page 87:

Answers will vary. Possible answers include: 1. ambling: walking or strolling slowly; adore: love something or someone; ardent: enthusiastic, eager, passionate 2. *Llama* begins with double *l*; *aardvark* begins with double *a*. 3. The poet spelled every *a*

word with double *a* and every *l* word with double *l*. 4. The llama and the aardvark went for a walk. They both said, "I love you," and decided to stay together forever.

Answers to Questions on Page 89

1. cornflakes 2. dish or wide dish 3. sifter or silver sifter 4. sugar
For student metaphors, accept almost any answer that makes sense. The child's answer should not use "like" or "as" to make the comparison. Sample answers: skeletons, hay, a ghost, swords, ice cream

Answers to Questions on Page 92

1. Poem #1: The poet thinks spaghetti is wonderful. Poem #2: The poet says her mom's spaghetti is the best. 2. Answers will vary. Poem #1: The speaker calls spaghetti "wonderful stuff," says "I can't get enough," and tells the spaghetti, "I love you a lot." Poem #2: The speaker says that her mom's spaghetti is the best. 3. In the second poem, the person doesn't get to eat the spaghetti because it is slippery and falls off of the fork. 4. Answers will vary. Possible answers include: In one poem the speaker eats the spaghetti, and in the other the speaker just talks about it. Students may also recognize that only the first poem mentions sauce and cheese.